Barrett

Administration
and
Management

Theory
and
Techniques

A Guide for
Practising Managers

Ina R. Barrett

Administration *and* Management

Theory *and* Techniques

A Guide for Practising Managers

authorHOUSE®

AuthorHouse™
1663 Liberty Drive
Bloomington, IN 47403
www.authorhouse.com
Phone: 1-800-839-8640

Published by AuthorHouse   03/19/2012

ISBN: 978-1-4685-6697-0 (sc)
ISBN: 978-1-4685-6696-3 (e)

CR

Dedicated to my children

Grace Anne Barrett-Baisden
Homer Burns Fitzgerald Barrett
Karelle Nicola Barrett-Sellers

"You are the wind beneath my wings."

CR

Contents

Contents

Contents

Acknowledgements

In acknowledging those persons who have influenced my decision to write this text on administration and management, I have to thank, firstly, past students in various disciplines throughout the Caribbean with whom I worked during my tenure as a lecturer in the Department of Government at The University of the West Indies (UWI). These mostly mature students, holding senior positions in their organizations, not only encouraged and prompted me to write, but they also motivated me by expressing appreciation for the knowledge gained in their courses, which they have been able to apply to their own management situations. This work has been, in large part, a response to those promptings, and I thank those who were able to convince me that writing the book was a good idea. From the writing of the book and recollecting of past experiences, I have derived much satisfaction, and for that I sincerely thank them.

I owe a debt of gratitude to Dr. Hermi Hewitt, formerly director of the UWI School of Nursing (UWISON), for the confidence she invested in me when she contracted me to teach a course in the MSc Nursing Administration programme, in academic years 2007 to 2010. That experience provided me with the academic and intellectual environment, which was the fillip I needed to continue and ultimately to complete the organization of the material which I had started some five years earlier. I also acknowledge with thanks the support I received from Mrs. Pauline Dawkins, nurse educator/administrator at UWISON, who was my course coordinator. Her assistance in recommending and locating relevant course material was highly valued.

I am extremely grateful to the following persons who have contributed to the preparation of various stages of the manuscript. I thank, firstly, Ms. Charmaine McKenzie, curriculum development specialist in the Open Campus, UWI (previously the UWI Distance Education Centre – UWIDEC), for reading and making valuable editorial comments on the content and organization of the manuscript. As in a previous work on administrative principles and practices, Ms. McKenzie provided timely guidance in every aspect of writing and presenting the written material for publication. All this she did at tremendous personal sacrifice, given her various other commitments, and for this I am deeply grateful to her.

I am extremely grateful to Ms. Donna Marks, communications specialist and professional editor, for contributing of her vast experience in editing academic material for government and non-profit organizations. She has been generous with her time and skill in editing and contributed valuable comments on the content of the book and suggestions on the design and layout. She also kept in touch by e-mail with other persons who were involved in the process.

My special thanks finally to Ms. Monica Dixon, formerly of the Printery, The University of the West Indies, whose word-processing skills and competence in translating barely legible manuscripts, took the written material from its embryonic stage to its final readiness for publication. I also thank Ms. Carole Thompson for so creatively applying her graphics and skills in designing the book.

To everyone–family, friends, and colleagues–who, by words of encouragement and many acts of kindness, have supported me in this effort, I say a big "Thank You".

Foreword

by Hermi H. Hewitt, OD, PhD, RN, RM, FAAN

I commend Dr. Barrett for investing the energy and tremendous effort to publish this comprehensive text on administration and management. I have collaborated with Dr. Barrett for over 23 years when she taught the course "Administrative Techniques" to students in the Advanced Nursing Administration Programme at The University of the West Indies. More recently, Dr. Barrett taught "Theoretical Perspectives in Nursing Administration" at The University of the West Indies, School of Nursing to students reading for the master of science in nursing administration.

In teaching administration and management, she used the experiential approach, which enabled students to apply the practical issues of their specialty in understanding the theories about which they were learning. This approach also allowed her to induce the critical thinking and evaluative processes of students to effectively use administrative techniques to meet workforce needs. Her teaching was supported by a number of cases, which she published in 2005 under the title *Organizational Challenges – a Caribbean Perspective*.

The skills and guidelines for developing management and administrative effectiveness are described in this book and reflect those practical experiences gained from the teaching and learning processes in which she engaged. This makes the book distinctive as it blends management and administrative thoughts with the views, opinions and examples gained from teaching and consulting in a wide cross-section of both private and public sector environments in several states in the English-speaking Caribbean while she was a lecturer in the Department of Government at The University of the West Indies.

Dr. Barrett has integrated these variables well while writing a valuable text that offers strategies and examples to address managerial and administrative issues relevant to any setting. This is a timeless work, which will be valuable to students pursuing any aspect of management or administration, in any setting or environment, while challenging the student and/or manager to develop new thoughts and ideas about the management of formal organizations.

Introduction

Administration and Management: Theory and Techniques (A Guide for Practising Managers) is designed to provide students of management and administration as well as practising managers with a comprehensive reference text on administrative management theories and their application to practice. It achieves this through a two-part structure that explores the subject matter under the headings Theories of Administration (Section 1) and Techniques of Administration and Management (Section 2).

Section 1 of the book traces the development of management thought, starting with early ideas of organization and significant events that have influenced conceptions of and changes in organizations over time. The major schools of management—the Classical, Neo-Classical, Human Relations (Behavioral), Decision-Making and Systems and Contingency—and their main proponents are outlined. For each school, its application and impact is discussed and the main concepts with which it is identified are examined. Criticisms or deficiencies of the theories are also highlighted as well as their relevance in today's technological and globalized working environment.

Section 2 of the book examines in depth the skills and techniques associated with management and administration, "providing a framework for the development of the knowledge and skills required to carry out the activities of management". The skills identified are conceptual, technical, human relations, and critical thinking skills, which connect to the tools or techniques used in the practice of management or administration and link directly to the theories covered in Section 1. The techniques examined are decision-making, planning, organizing, directing (commanding), and controlling (evaluating), and these are outlined in a practical and straightforward manner.

The division of the book into two sections allows the reader to gain a comprehensive understanding of the theories as well as a broad-based, experiential overview of how the techniques can be translated effectively in any work environment.

In today's technological and globalized environment, organizational change takes place at a faster pace than it did during the earlier periods of the development of management thought. There is a popular and well-accepted axiom that says "without change, there can be no growth and development". The book also proposes some techniques and strategies for the management of time, which is an important area of study, and for which there was no well-developed theory in early management thought. To help practitioners to effectively manage change in their organizations, the book identifies the factors that lead to change, steps in the change process, types of change managers, and ways of responding to change in organizations. This is followed by an outline of the techniques for managing change.

With the exponential growth in the literature on organization and management strategies for solving organizational problems, as well as new methodologies for accessing information relevant to specific organizational contexts, what the practising manager needs, and this text attempts to provide, is a base from which to begin to understand some of the root causes of organizational problems and to move towards finding practical solutions to those problems. Online resources for further study are identified at the end of each chapter; these should be seen as indicative of the vast amount of information available on the Internet, which must be approached critically by the student or the practitioner of management.

This book has applicability to a wide range of management and administrative environments, including nursing, public health and other health-related fields, the security services and a wide range of government and quasi-government agencies, private sector organizations and non-profit organizations (NGOs).

It is my experience in the diverse and multifaceted administrative cultures of the English-speaking Caribbean that has enabled me to bring together in this text the science and art of administration and management.

The Development of Modern Management Thought

Historical Overview

Historical records show that management thought has been developing over many centuries. These records reveal that some form of management has always existed wherever co-operative effort was necessary for the survival of groups of people. For example, documents found from Sumerian civilization of around 5000 BC provided evidence that Sumerian temple priests managed great wealth—flocks, herds, revenues and estates—through an intricate system of tax collection and record keeping. The accounts of the building of the great pyramids of Egypt (from 5000 BC to 525 BC) are a demonstration of the organizational capabilities of that civilization.

The records of Babylonia and Hebrew nations have also left us with examples of the practice of management in those civilizations. The records of ancient China, Greece and Rome show that formal organizations with strict rules and regulations and a rigid authority structure have always existed. Evidence of the long and effective management that has persisted for centuries and, up to the present time, can also be found in the records and practices of the Roman Catholic Church, stands as a monument to the durability of medieval management practices.

From the earliest times, military organizations have practised management principles. Notable among them are the military exploits of Alexander the Great, who successfully led vast armies across Europe, through the use of staffing principles that remain in use to the present time.

Throughout the ages, philosophers and historians contributed to the development of management thought, but their views and ideas were mostly unhinged and unconnected and did not constitute a systematic theory of management. The entire record of thoughts on management that covered the early period shows a lack of continuity. Several of the so-called 'new' management principles were indeed ideas that had been written and practised for centuries. Similarly, some of the errors made in one civilization were repeated over and over again.

However, major changes in the course of economic history had a significant impact on the development of management thought and indeed laid a foundation for the development of modern management theory.

The First Industrial Revolution

Between 1700 and the late 18th century, during the first Industrial Revolution in England, a new generation of practising managers emerged. Their interest was primarily in the development of new ideas and methods of organizing the factors of production to meet the challenges brought about by fundamental changes in the economy. In this period was laid the foundation for the development of diverse strands of management thought, with various perspectives, all purporting to provide managers with the capability to manage their organizations more efficiently.

During that period, the classical economist Adam Smith theorized about the value of the application of the principle of specialization or division of labour to the manufacturing of goods. Around 1776, he published the well-known work titled *An Inquiry into the Nature and Cause of the Wealth of Nations*. By the end of the 18th century, economists on the other side of the Atlantic Ocean—Thomas Jefferson, Eli Whitney, James Watts, to name a few—also were making significant contributions to the development of management thought as it applied to large-scale organizations. Despite the emergence of these ideas and several written works, up to that time it could not be said that a school of management thought had developed. Another century had to pass before such a development took place.

In the 1800s, the literature on management grew under the influence of the large number of individuals who are known as classical economists. Concepts about management functions and principles were being developed and the foundation was solidly laid in that period for the development of the classical theories of management thought. Charles Babbage, who pioneered the development of the first digital computer, was one well-known writer. His famous work on the Economy of Machinery and Manufacturing was published in 1832. It contained elements of scientific management, emphasized specialization, division of labour, motion and time study, cost accounting. He even studied such details as the effect of tints of paper and colours of ink on employees' efficiency.

The Second Industrial Revolution

During the second half of the 19th century, the second Industrial Revolution began, this time in the United States of America. This revolution was brought about by the expansion in the machine industry, which had spread from Europe. This phenomenon, coupled with the abolition of slavery, which made forced labour a scarce commodity, created a shift in the balance between labour and capital. Again, managers on the American side of the Atlantic Ocean were confronted with the problems of having to manage large-scale operations, employing capital-intensive methods of production without any well-developed theory of management. The managers of businesses were mainly industrial engineers and, in their search for solutions, formed themselves into associations and societies where they discussed their problems, presented papers and published their views in professional journals. Their thoughts on management were naturally directed to such matters as the management of railroads and other related industrial enterprises.

Some of the areas of concern of these managers were the improvement in the organization of materials, division of labour, efficiency in the use of time and the development of appropriate wage systems. Not much attention was given to the management of people, except to ensure that they gave a fair day's work for a fair day's pay. The harsh management practices of the day were almost inhuman and were justified, ironically, on the philosophy of Protestantism, which argued that man was responsible for his own destiny and that hard work and thrift and self-reliance were the real virtues.

The Modern Era

At the turn of the 20th century, management thought was emerging from being a disorganized and nebulous group of concepts to becoming a field of study with set principles by which managers could be guided. The century that followed saw a virtual explosion in the development of management thought. The earliest group of thinkers has been referred to as classical theorists and their views, which were developed in this context, were preceded by others of an earlier period. But they were the first to develop a systematic body of ideas; and they laid a foundation on which modern management theory has been built. Some of the events in history that were major catalysts for change in the development of management thought were the two World Wars (1914–1918 and 1939–1945) and the Great Depression of the late 1920s and early 1930s.

During **World War I**, industrial psychologists carried out research on the effect of psychological factors (eg, fatigue) on worker productivity. These researchers laid the foundation for the experiments on which human relations theories were built.

The Great Depression of the late 1920s shook the foundation of society and showed up problems that, up to then, had not even been considered. Many members of the hitherto wealthy classes became the new poor and were unable to provide for themselves. Out of this situation emerged the notion of the Positive State, the Social Ethic and, in some countries, the Welfare State. The view in this new philosophy is that the state, and not business interests, had to take the lead in social and economic activities. The management of government and the discipline of public administration took on a more prominent role from which new theories of public administration developed.

World War II gave rise to the importance of the quantitative school of management thought. This school—also referred to as Operation Research, Operational Research and Management Science—brought together several disciplines (eg, mathematics, physical science, economics) to bear on the study and solution of management problems. Although this approach to problem solving had a long history, it was not widely applied until the time of World War II, when it was used in the improvement of war-time activities (eg, anti-aircraft gunnery, anti-submarine warfare, determining convoy size and conduct of bombing raids). After the war, the approach was introduced in business operations and later brought into management. This approach, which became known as the Systems Approach, opened new vistas for the development of management thought.

Conclusion

This historical overview of the development of modern management thought is by no means exhaustive. Many of the important thinkers throughout the ages have not been included. Also, the diverse strands of ideas did not emerge in any logical sequence. Indeed, there have been areas of overlap and all so-called 'new' ideas have their roots in the past.

In the process of the development of modern management thought, different schools of thought have emerged. Within each school, individual or groups of theorists have emphasized diverse perspectives or approaches to management. While some of these views are similar, others are different and, in some instances, might even be contradictory. However, the theories that were developed between the late 19th and mid-20th century laid a foundation for management that is being practised in the present era. The schools of management thought briefly represented in this text are as follows:

- The Classical School

- The Neoclassical School

- The Human Relations or Behavioral School

- The Decision-Making School

- The Systems and Contingency School

By the end of the 20th century, growth in technology brought about radically new meaning to the concept of the 'organization' or 'the firm' for which management theories were originally developed. Modern management thinkers such as Peter Drucker and Alvin Toffler have predicted a future for management that goes beyond the 20th century. They have envisaged that 'bureaucracy' as a management structure was endangered and that factory methods of production would become obsolete. The turbulent social and economic times through which the world is now passing are revealed as part of the inevitable changes that will affect management in the future. However, these predictions and revelations do not in any way suggest that managers in the present era will completely abandon the principles and practices of management, which developed from the late 19th century to mid 20th century.

References

Chapman, S.D. (1967) *The Early Factory Masters*, p.41 (David Charles, London).

Checkland, S. (1964) *The Rise of Industrial Society*, 1815-1885, p.120, (Longmans, London).

George, Claude S. (1972) *The History of Management Thought,* 2nd ed. (Prentice Hall, Englewood Cliffs, NJ).

Hobsbawn, E.J. (1962) *The Age of Revolution,* p. 48. (Weidenfeld Nicolson, London).

Lupton, Tom (1983) *Management and the Social Sciences,* 3rd ed. (Penguin Books Ltd., London).

Massie, Joseph L. (1971) *Essentials of Management,* 2nd ed., pp. 12-14 (Prentice Hall, Englewood Cliffs, NJ).

Nef, J.V (1954) "The Progress of Technology and the Growth of Large Scale Industry", in E. Carus Wilson, Ed. *Essays in Economy History*, pp. 88-107 (Arnold, London).

Online Resource

Historical and Contemporary Theories of Management http://managementhelp.org/management/theories.htm

The Classical Schools

Introduction

The theorists identified in this school are referred to as 'classical' because they were the first to set out systematically a body of thought that would guide managers in their effort to achieve higher levels of efficiency in the management of people, money and material.

Three management theorists from the Classical School have been selected for special consideration:

- **Frederick Winslow Taylor** is the well-known name associated with Scientific Management Perspective, which includes the 'one best way' of managing;

- **Max Weber** developed the Structural Perspective in management in his focus on 'bureaucracy', sometimes referred to as an 'ideal' type of management;

- **Henri Fayol** is associated with the Administrative Management Perspective, which includes the six elements and 14 principles of management.

The development of each perspective has been influenced by environmental and other conditions that shaped the thoughts and ideas of the theorists. Consideration of these factors is critical to any analysis or evaluation of their applicability to the management of modern organizations.

Scientific Management Perspectives

Frederick Winslow Taylor (1856–1915), who has been referred to as "the father of scientific management", was a relatively unknown engineer from Philadelphia, Pennsylvania, United States, when he started his management career. In 1878, he was appointed pattern maker at the Midvale Iron Works, from which position he rose to chief engineer in 1884 at the early age of 28. It was Taylor's observant and naturally enthusiastic approach, which he brought to every activity in which he was involved, that led him to develop a 'scientific' approach to the management of the factory.

Taylor observed that there was no rational method of assigning workers to their jobs and that they were often placed in jobs for which they did not have either the ability or the aptitude. This ad-hoc placement system provided opportunity for workers to find ways of idling while creating the impression that they were busy—an activity referred as systematic soldering.

He also found that there was no coordination between departments, hence work flow was inconsistent, work sometimes flowing too fast, causing bottlenecks or at other times too slowly causing backlogs in the production process.

He observed that factory managers did not possess good decision-making skills. They made decisions, for the most part, on the basis of past experience, 'rule-of-thumb' evaluations or on intuition. He also found that managers had no clear idea of the difference between their responsibilities and those of the workers. In practice, workers were performing functions that were clearly managerial and many decisions were subjected to the whims and fancies of the workers. He realized that, while industrialists were knowledgeable about the efficiency of the machine, they had no concept of the efficiency of the worker. Consequently, inefficiency in factory management was as much the result of poor work practices as from the lack of employers' management skills.

Based on these observations, Taylor set out to develop a science of management. His first area of concern was to develop a standard by which the efficiency of the worker could be assessed and to use this standard as a measure for all workers doing the same job. To achieve this standard setting, from which all activities directed towards achieving efficiency would flow, Taylor proceeded to work on four basic principles.

The first principle was to find *one best way of doing a job*. This involved gathering all the information he could from the knowledge that workers had in their heads—their traditional ways of doing things, which they had accumulated over the years. This information was later recorded, tabulated and reduced to laws and mathematical formulae. By so doing, he was able to find the one best way of doing a job, and, consequently, the quantity and quality of job performance would improve.

The second principle was finding *the best person for the job*. This involved the scientific selection and progressive development of the manual worker. This included studying his character, his temperament, the manner of his performance, his limitations and his potential for development. By this process, it could be discovered if a worker was not performing according to standard, whether he or she could be retrained or should be dismissed from the job. Systematic on-the-job training would also be part of this process.

The third principle was marrying the *science of doing the job with the scientifically selected and trained worker*. This would involve the payment of incentives in the form of higher wages to the best workers. This system of incentive payment would result in improved productivity and relieve the foreman and his 'whip-persuasion' role.

The fourth principle was the (almost) equal division of the actual work of the establishment between managers and workers. He saw the need for good supervision and developed the concept of the *functional foremanship* with specialists employed in every phase of supervision to ensure excellence in operation. This new principle of managing through sharing meant that there had to be close cooperation between the two sides.

Application of the Scientific Principles

Taylor tested these principles in an experiment at Bethlehem Steel, where he was working as a consultant engineer to management. As he tested his principles, he discovered that there was increased efficiency. It was possible under the new method to decrease the number of workers needed to do a job, to increase the daily earnings of the workers and to save money for the firm.

Taylor stated that his four principles of management, which constituted Scientific Management, were more that an efficiency device. He stressed the point that Scientific Management was both conceptual and philosophical and involved a complete mental revolution on the part of the management of the organization, as well as on the part of the working man. It was incumbent on the working man to have a new mental attitude to his work. It also required an equally complete revolution on the part of management (including foremen, superintendents, business owners and the board of directors) to have a new mental attitude towards their fellow managers, towards their workers and towards their daily tasks.

Although Taylor's ideas may now seem commonplace, his concepts about management and the worker were revolutionary in his time. Following are some of the problems that he identified:

- The lack of standardized methods of performing routine tasks.
- The archaic and irrational decision-making methods used by managers—they were based mainly on intuition and judgment, precedents and past experiences.
- The lack of distinction between the roles and responsibilities of managers and those of labour.
- The absence of any structured method of reward that would be an incentive for motivating the workers.

Impact of Scientific Management

Impact on Management

Taylor's approach had a direct positive impact on management in the following areas:

- Improvement in the general outlay of the 'shop' and the attendant improvement in factory management
- More effective and efficient utilization of equipment, labour and raw material

Concommittantly, management became more effective in achieving its goals and improving profit margins. It also improved its corporate image and consequently was able to increase its competitiveness in the marketplace. Such management principles as research, planning, standard-setting and controlling were integrated into management processes.

Impact on Labour

Labour also benefitted from the introduction of scientific management.

- The introduction of incentive payment attached to productivity provided better opportunities for workers to increase their wages and, consequently, to improve their living conditions.

- Workers enjoyed more reliable job placements and better working conditions.

- Employees' working hours were also more consistent and their tenure less uncertain.

Some Negative Responses

Despite its generally positive impact, Scientific Management has been harshly criticized. In the early years, the new approach to management and workers was cited for lacking consideration for the workers. For example, some of the methods used to achieve the goals of efficiency were considered harsh, in human terms. These included very close supervision, with the employers monitoring every movement of the workers and the altering of rest pauses, changes in the lighting and frequent changes in lunch periods and the length of time worked.

These changes and dislocations were unwelcomed by both workers and supervisors, who saw the interventions as unnecessary interference. Some workers regarded the experiments as exploitation and many lost their jobs to redundancy as a result of more efficient production techniques and uses of human resources.

Taylor, for his part, had a negative view of trade unions. He accused them of encouraging workers to use restrictive practices, which, in his view, worked against the interests of the workers as they prevented them from maximizing their earning capacity. Needless to say, the trade union leaders resented Taylor's influence over management. Of course, any reduction in the size of the workforce was also seen as having a negative impact on the size of trade union membership. Over time, Scientific Management has been subjected to some criticisms, especially by the organizational humanists. They regarded this approach as lacking in consideration for the workers who, they said, were regarded as no more than cogs in a machine.

Summary and Conclusions

Although Taylor's ideas may seem commonplace now, his concepts about the management of the worker and the workplace were novel in his time. The principles of Scientific Management became widely accepted in industrial enterprises throughout the United States of America and the idea of finding the 'one best way' of doing the job become the standard for achieving efficiency. By the end of World War I (1914–1918), interest in scientific management had spread to Europe, France, Italy and Germany—and as far as Japan. Through Taylor's work, other experimenters were inspired to develop scientific methods of managing people at work.

Notably among them were Frank and Lillian Gilbreth, who refined the concepts of 'time and motion' studies, which was first introduced by Taylor. Some aspects of Scientific Management have remained relevant to the management of large-scale organizations. The general principles of standardization of processes are still being applied in the mass production of goods and in the performance of a wide range of services. There is wide usage of the principle of selecting the right person for the job and placing the person in a job where he or she is best able to perform efficiently.

The recently developed concept of Total Quality Management (TQM), which focuses on the improvement of quality, cost reduction because of less re-work of jobs, making fewer mistakes and better use of machine time and materials, is based largely on Scientific Management.

On the other hand, some aspects of Taylor's management principles are not applicable to modern management practices. For example, managers in the 21st century have to involve their subordinates in the decision-making process. In fact, with the advances in technology, finding the 'one best way' of doing a job is outdated. Reliance on management to determine the content of a job or the way of doing the job would stifle creativity and cause organizations to lose their competitive edge.

The Structural Perspective

Max Weber (1864–1920) was a contemporary of Frederick Taylor and Henri Fayol, two classical theorists. But his contribution to classical management theory came from a different vantage point. Weber was a German scholar whose work had a great influence on modern sociology. He was not a practising manager, as were the other two theorists aforementioned, and he was sometimes referred to as an 'armchair theorist'. As a student of history, he wrote about the many forms of social organization and he theorized about the reason for their emergence as well as their decline. His observations led him to conclude that there were three related concepts that influenced the process of managing human society.

His analysis of comparative social systems led him to conclude that each system was maintained by the interplay of three related concepts: power, authority and legitimacy:

Power was defined by Weber as the possibility that a person within a social relationship will be in a position to carry out his will, despite resistance, regardless of the basis on which that possibility lies and irrespective of consequences. Power can be exercised, for example, by coercion and the capacity to use force.

Authority (also referred to as domination) is redefined as a form of power. The difference, however, between power and authority is that in the authority relationship there is a system of beliefs and agreements between those giving an order and those who carry out the order. This system of beliefs gives the ruler the right to issue the order and the followers the duty to obey without questioning.

Legitimacy Weber explains that through a process of socialization, individuals in a society learn that the beliefs held by ruler and ruled are right and acceptable, and this system of beliefs gives legitimacy to the exercise of authority.

Authority Structures

According to Weber, as societies passed through the various stages of development, variations of belief systems and, consequently, of authority structures became idealized. He identified three ideal types of authority structures and the system of beliefs by which authority was legitimated.

1. Traditional authority rests on the belief in the sacredness of the social order as it has always existed. One example of this is the notion of "the divine right of kings".

2. Charismatic authority is legitimated on the belief that the ruler (or leader) has the "gifts of grace"—spiritual or magical powers given by God, whomever he may be construed to be.

3. Rational legal authority is not owed to anyone personally, but rests on the rationally enacted rules and regulations that specify to whom and to what rule people owe obedience. The legitimating factor in this case is the belief in the rightness of the law and on technical expertise

He further explains that each authority structure has its own type of administrative apparatus through which the activities of the society are managed.

Traditional authority structure is managed either through

- *Patrimonial form* of administration, in which administrative staff is made up of personal retainers, relatives, favourites, servants, etc. or

- *Feudal form* of administration, in which administrative staff is made up of converts, allies or loyalists who really believe that they owe allegiance to the leader.

Charismatic authority structure is served through the personal devotion of followers, with no expectation of reward.

Rational-legal authority structure is the most modern structure of social organization and, according to Weber's formulation, is best managed by an administrative apparatus referred to as a 'bureaucracy'.

Weber's Model of Bureaucracy

According to Weber, the rational-legal system, which is the most modern system of social organization, is best managed by the administrative apparatus referred to as a 'bureaucracy'. Weber believed that the main features or characteristics of a bureaucracy, which are likely to achieve the highest level of efficiency, are as follows:

- A clear-cut *division of labour,* which makes it possible to employ specialists to carry out official duties.

- A clearly *defined hierarchy of offices,* in which each lower office is subject to the control of the next higher office.

- Offices or posts should be filled through a *free contractual agreement.* The authority to which staff is subjected must be limited to their impersonal obligations, and should not extend beyond life inside the organization.

- Officials should be subject to a strict and consistent *system of rules* in the conduct of their official duties.

- The official should conduct his or her duties in a *spirit of formalistic impersonality.* He or she should display neither fear nor favour in a relationship with either other officials or the public he or she serves.

- Appointments to positions in the bureaucracy should be made on the basis of *technical competence* and the official is protected against arbitrary dismissal.

- The job should constitute a career and there should be a *system of promotion,* which should be based on seniority or merit, or both.

- Officials should be *remunerated by a fixed salary* in money, and should, for the most part, have the right to a pension.

- The office should be treated as the sole or at least the *primary occupation* of the incumbent.

- The official should work entirely separated from the *ownership of the means of administration* and cannot appropriate or bequeath the position.

This model of the bureaucracy has been referred to as Weber's 'ideal type', although this was not Weber's opinion. The construct represents Weber's concept of a rational system of administration. That is to say that each element of the structure has the capacity to contribute to the persistence and effective operation of the organization. While Weber was not unaware of some of the contradictions in the construct, he did not take his analysis beyond the point of looking at the functions of the various elements.

Criticisms of Bureaucratic Model

In looking at Weber's theory some writers have pointed out that there is another side of the bureaucratic form of administration. Robert Merton, in his book *Social Theory and Social Structure* (1957), referred to the dysfunctions of bureaucracy, which means that the same bureaucratic features that can lead to efficiency also can lead to inefficiency. Here are some examples:

- Rules exist so that there will be reliability and predictability in the organization's structures and processes. But rules often lack flexibility and encourage a tendency for bureaucrats to see rules as ends in themselves rather than means to an end. In many instances, bureaucratic red tape and overemphasis on rules can be the cause of much organizational inefficiency and delay. While rules set out the steps to be followed in a particular process, they can be dysfunctional in a crisis situation in which the official might need to omit some of the steps in order to get to a quick solution. When rules are being made, some provision has to be made for creativity and initiative to avoid the dysfunctional effects of the rules. Furthermore, very often there are no existing rules to deal with a new situation or a rule that exists is outdated. The bureaucrat who is 'rule-bound' can be a liability rather than an asset to the organization.

- A rigid hierarchical structure could stifle initiative in decision-making and, hence, affect efficiency. Traditional managers often insist that the chain of command be strictly adhered to at all times. Any deviation could lead to the use of sanctions. So, while the hierarchy is for the distribution of authority and responsibility and function to identify the centre of accountability, it can also have the dysfunctional effect of stifling creativity, particularly at lower levels of the organization.

11

- While division of labour specialization can lead to the development of proficiency, overspecialization can be dysfunctional. The size of the organization and the amount of staff available to perform the required functions can be an obstacle to specialization. This would clearly by dysfunctional to efficiency and effectiveness. In these situations team work is more to be desired that division of labour or specialization.

- Impersonality is a feature of the bureaucracy that, theoretically, is intended to ensure that everyone receives equal treatment, but can also cause inequalities in its application. Persons seeking assistance from the bureaucracy have different experiences and different needs. Some persons may require more personalized attention because of some individual disadvantages or challenges, such as the level of literacy, economic means and social background. In the interest of effectiveness, bureaucrats may need these persons in order to give some personalized attention and redress some of the imbalances among the clientele.

- Security of tenure may also lead to bureaucratic weakness in instances where retaining the post is given more importance than the service for which the post is created. Bureaucratic security can lead individuals to give "one year's service twenty times over than to give twenty years service". It is sometimes considered more important to obey the rules and avoid conflict in order to receive a favourable confidential report. (This bureaucratic weakness is now being exposed under administrative reform and officers are required to achieve goals and objectives instead of being judged on subjective criteria).

Despite some criticisms of the bureaucratic model, it has persisted as the structure used in the administration of large-scale organizations over several decades. However, dysfunctions that have been identified have led to many structural adjustments and administrative reforms to meet the demands of a new era.

Summary and Conclusions

Max Weber, unlike Frederick Taylor, was not a practising manager. His theory was developed from a historical perspective and his observations about the management of organizations were made from outside. His focus was on the structure of organizations, the contribution that a particular structure (the bureaucracy) makes to the achievement of efficiency.

Weber was not a passionate advocate of his theory, as were the other two theorists discussed in their classical school. However, in his analysis, he posited the view that organizations that were structured on bureaucratic principles were likely to achieve the highest level of efficiency.

A comprehensive enunciation of the dysfunction was given by Robert Merton in his *Social Theory and Social Theory* (1957). This work examined some of the ways in which some bureaucratic features can have negative effects on efficiency as well as on organizational effectiveness.

On the other hand, some characteristics of the bureaucracy have been found to be timeless and the managers have been cautioned not to be so anxious to overturn the bureaucratic model, lest they "throw out the baby with the bath water".

Administrative Management Perspective

Henri Fayol (1841–1925), a French industrialist and a contemporary of Frederick Taylor, represents the first attempt to grapple with general management principles. He has been referred to as the "real father of classical management theory", while others have claimed that he is the "father of modern management thought".

Fayol was formally educated first at Lycee de Lyons and then at the National School of Mines at St. Etienne. In 1860, he graduated at age 19 as a mining engineer and was appointed as engineer to the Fourchambault Coal Mining Company. In 1888, he became the managing director of the company. He retired from the position in 1918. He remained a director of the company until his death in December 1925 at the age of 84.

It was his work experience and his long and successful career as a manager of an industrial organization that formed the basis of Fayol's writings and the development of a theory for the management of a large-scale organization. His main concern was with the problems that managers faced; and he set out to provide an explicit and broad framework of the general principles of management. His major work in this regard was his famous *General and Industrial Management,* which was first published in French in 1916. Due to the intervening years of World War I (1914–1918), his book was not widely available in English until 1949. However, the content of his theory is a template for management training worldwide, even today.

Activities of Industrial Concerns

Fayol divided the activities or essential functions of industrial concerns into six groups:

1. Technical activities (production, manufacture, adaptation)
2. Commercial activities (buying, selling, exchange)
3. Financial activities (search for and optimum use of capital)
4. Security activities (protection of property and persons)
5. Accounting activities (stocktaking, balance sheets, costs, statistics)
6. Managerial activities (including planning, organizing, commanding, coordinating controlling).

It was Fayol's view that these six groups of activities are essential for the functioning of all undertakings, whether they were large or small, simple or complex. But while the first five sets of activities are self-explanatory, or require only the minimum amount of explanation, the sixth, (ie, the managerial group) requires further explanation.

The first five sets of activities are usually carried out by personnel who are trained to operate in their own sphere of competence and who, more often than not, have no knowledge of the internal working of the other group. At the same time, all these activities have overlapping relevance and the overall efficiency of the entire organization is dependent on the effective operation of each set of activities.

The responsibility for ensuring that each set of activities, while performing independent functions, is also operating in an interdependent relationship with each other falls under the purview of managerial activities.

Functions of Management

The five elements or essential functions of the management activities as defined by Fayol are as follows:

Planning

Fayol explained that managing means looking ahead or 'prevoyance'. Thus, planning holds a priority place in the business of managing an enterprise. It includes assessing the future and making provision for it. A plan of action must include the result that is envisaged as well as the line of action to be followed and the means of attaining the end result. To be effective, a plan should be dynamic, that is, it must include provision for change to be made, as necessary. It must contain levity and precision as well as flexibility and provision for continuity. The plan must have as much accuracy as to be compatible with unknown factors bearing on the fate of the business. Planning must be based on continuous research.

Organizing

Fayol was concerned with both the structure and processes of organization. He summarized organizing as providing a business with everything useful to its functioning—raw materials, tools, capital, personnel—and suggested that these provisions fell into two main categories or groups:

- the material organization and
- the human organization.

With regard to the structure and process of organization, he emphasized the necessity for a clear definition of objectives, authority, responsibility, decisions and tasks and selection and training of managers. One of the central themes in Fayol's discussion of organization is the scalar chain or the gradations of authority in an organization by which supreme authority becomes effective throughout the entire structure. His opinion was that each superior should have a "span of control", comprising no more than four or five immediate subordinates and that there should be an organization chart specifying the distribution of authority.

Commanding

Fayol argued that everyone in a position of leadership is responsible for getting the optimum return from all employees in a particular unit, in the interest of the whole concern. For the manager, that is the object of command, and persons in a managerial position should attempt to make unity, energy and initiative a strong feature of their respective units. This must be done through example, knowledge of the business, knowledge of the subordinates, continuous contact with staff and a broad view of the directing function. In this way, the manager maintains a high level of activity by instilling a sense of mission in the subordinates.

Coordinating

Fayol's definition of coordination is to "harmonize all the activities of a concern, so as to facilitate its proper working and its success". Coordination is necessary to bind together, unify and harmonize all the activities and efforts that are involved in the performance of the various organizational tasks. This can be achieved only through the continuous flow of information, and the general manager achieves this objective through regular meetings between heads of units. This process keeps the general manager informed about important management issues that allow him or her to make decisions and give orders on matters concerning many departments.

Controlling

"To control", according to Fayol, "is seeing that everything occurs in conformity with the established rules and expressed commands", and the object of control is to point out weaknesses and errors in order and prevent their recurrence. To be effective, control must be exercised in a timely manner, and there must be a system of sanctions in place for nonperformance. The best way to ensure that control is carried out effectively is to separate all functions concerned with inspection from the operations of departments whose work they inspect.

Fayol drew on his own experience as a successful manager to develop a number of general principles of management. Although he did not assume that these principles had universal application or any permanence, they have become part of management thought and have been widely accepted as fundamental tenets.

Principles of Management

Following are the 14 principles of management that Fayol outlined:

1. **Division of Labour**—This is recognized as the best means of making use of individuals and groups. The object of the division of work is to produce more and better work with the same effort. (Of course, this has its limits, which experience and a sense of proportion teach us must not be exceeded).

2. **Authority and Responsibility**—Authority is the right to command and the power to exact obedience. Statutory authority has to be distinguished from personal authority and, for good leadership, personal authority is the essential complement of statutory authority. Wherever authority is exercised responsibility follows. The ability to apply sanction is also an important factor.

3. **Discipline**—Fayol regarded discipline as a set of conventions established between the organization and its employees. It is absolutely essential for the smooth running of the organization. In order to have effective discipline, the following things should be present:

   - First-class leadership
   - Agreements that are fair and easily understood
   - Judicious use of sanctions

4. **Unity of Command**—No person should receive orders from more than one superior. People cannot bear dual command—it is a source of conflict in human association.

5. **Unity of Direction**—There should be one head and one plan for a group of activities having the same objectives. Unity of direction should not be confused with unity of command. Unity of direction is provided by sound organization of the body corporate. Unity of command relates to the functioning of personnel and the giving of orders.

6. **Subordination of Private Interest to the General Good**—The interests of an employee or group of employees should not prevail over the interest of the whole organization.

7. **Staff Remuneration**—Pay should be fair and, as far as possible, provide satisfaction both to employer and employee. Such concepts as time rates, job rates, price rates, and nonfinancial incentives are discussed within this principle.

8. **Centralization**—This is a matter of proportion; in itself, it is neither good nor bad. The aim must be to find the point of balance between centralization and decentralization that gives the best overall results. The objective to be pursued is the optimum utilization of all faculties of the personnel.

9. **Scalar Chain**—This is sometimes referred to as the chain of command. Authority relationships should be followed, unless superiors have authorized their subordinates to communicate across authority lines. This principle, which satisfies the need for unity of command, can create delay in the execution of activities. As an alternative, Fayol recommends the use of the 'gang plank', whereby officers on the same level can communicate without going through the supervisor. (However, this requires that the superior be informed of the break in the chain as soon as possible).

10. **Order**—"A place for everything (everyone) and everything in its place." However, the place must be well chosen, otherwise there will be only a mere appearance of order and a papering over of disorder. Cleanliness is a corollary of orderliness and there is no appointed place for dirt. Human arrangement is made easier with a chart or plan; and a good system for selection of personnel is also very important.

11. **Stability of Tenure**—A stable workforce is to be encouraged. Unnecessary staff turnover is both the cause and effect of bad management. An employee should have enough time to get used to a new job and an opportunity to learn to do it well.

12. **Equity**—This results from a combination of kindliness and justice, but does not exclude forcefulness or sternness. People aspire to fair treatment and this must be recognized when dealing with staff.

13. **Initiative**—This implies the capacity to conceive a plan and then see it successfully executed. Opportunity for the exercise of initiative is a most powerful human stimulus but this opportunity must lie within the limits implied by respect and authority.

14. **Esprit de Corps**—This points to the need for teamwork and the importance of communication in obtaining it. There should be meetings between staff and verbal communication is to be desired over written.

Fayol saw these principles as being flexible and capable of adaptation to every need. They should have universal validity and be applicable to all types of administrations.

Summary and Conclusions

Henri Fayol, often referred to as the father of modern management theory, developed his views from the perspective of a senior manager in a large industrial organization. He applied his own caveat to his theories by stating that his 'principles' were capable of adaptation to different needs and situations.

Although his views were an important pioneering work, they contained some ambiguities. For instance, the distinction he makes between activities, elements and principles lack clarity and, under examination, his definitions of his principles are inadequate. Also, he does not give sufficient attention to human relations concepts, such as motivation and the behavior of individuals in organizations. Some of his principles are contradictory (eg, specialization—a principle—will increase the number of departments but this could cause problems of coordination, which is an important aspect of the elements of management).

Notwithstanding all this, Fayol's impact on the practice and theory of management cannot be overemphasized. His conceptual framework is still widely used and provides a platform on which modern management theory has been developed.

References

Blau, Peter M. and Meyer, M. (1987) *Bureaucracy in Modern Society*, 3rd ed. (McGraw Hill Publishing Co. New York).

Cole, G.A. (1990) *Management: Theory and Practice*, ELBS, 3rd ed., pp. 10-33 (DP Publications, London).

Etzioni, Amitai (1969) *A Sociological Reader on Complex Organization*, 2nd ed. (Holt, Rinehart and Winston, New York).

Fayol Henri (1974) *General & Industrial Administration* (Pitman Publishing, London).

Merton, Robert (1968) *Social Theory and Social Structure*, 3rd ed. (The Free Press, New York).

Mouzelis, N.P. (1975) *Organization and Bureaucracy: Analysis of Modern Theories,* revised edition (Routledge & Kegan Paul, London).

Pugh, D.S. (1970 *Organization Theory, Selected Readings*, new edition. (Penguin Business, London).

Pugh, D.S. and Hickson, D.J. (1989) *Writers on Organization*, 4th ed. (Harmondsworth, Penguin).

Taylor, F.W. (1947) *Scientific Management* (Harper & Row, New York).

Weber, Max (1947) "Legitimate Authority & Bureaucracy", from *The Theory of Social & Economic Organization*, translated and edited by A.M. Henderson and T. Parson, pp. 328-340 (Free Press, New York).

Online Resource

What is Organization Theory? www.oup.com/uk/orc/bin/9780199260218/hatch_ch01.pdf

The Neoclassical School

Introduction

The development of management theory passed from the classical school into what has been described as a 'neoclassical' phase, in which thinkers modified some of the more simplistic and idealistic notions of rationality. In particular, they looked more closely at the role of people in organizations. Not that the classical theorists gave no thought to people, but in their theories it was implied, if not stated, that people in organizations would automatically carry out the orders issued to them by managers. Frederick Taylor developed Scientific Management on the assumption that workers would work willingly and efficiently if they understood the relationship between their work and the company's ability to reward them adequately. In Max Weber's bureaucratic model of administration, it was assumed that the rational structures designed by managers would provide sufficient bases for the subordinates to obey instructions.

While neoclassical theorists held some of the same beliefs as the classicists, they were among the first to examine the way people in organizations would respond to the mechanistic approaches to management that were developed in the scientific, administrative and structural perspectives. In this respect, they formed the vanguard of the human relations movement. Three theorists whose views have been classified in this category are Mary Parker Follett, Chester Barnard and Elton Mayo.

Mary Parker Follet: 1863–1933

Follet, whose areas of study included philosophy, law and political science, was one of the first thinkers to recognize the need to consider the human factor in the management of organizations. She challenged the classical/traditional approaches in which it was assumed that if adequate structures were established through which authority would be exercised, then authority would automatically be accepted. In disagreeing with this view, Follet focused on the way in which conflict is resolved in formal organizations. The understanding is that, where people have to work together in a supervisor-subordinate relationship there would be conflict, because not everyone would have the same views about a problem. It is also a fact that there is always a difference in the amount of power that each person has in a conflict situation.

Conflict Resolution

Follet described the traditional method of conflict resolution as domination. In this method, one individual or group will possess the power of the hierarchical structure to force subordinates to carry out their wishes. Inherent in the power of the hierarchy is the capacity to apply sanctions or other coercive force. This method has weaknesses, not least of which are the negative feelings that subordinates have about their lack of power. This can, of course, result in individuals not putting out their best effort, and even when it appears that the conflict is resolved, it will keep surfacing from time to time.

The second method of conflict resolution is the use of the 'balance of power'. In this process, there is no obviously dominant power figure who has the statutory authority to force others to act in accordance with his or her wishes. However, in a process of negotiations and a trade-off of views or opinions, individuals or groups will compromise their position. Whether in the interest of time or in deference to some others holding informal power, there might be reluctance to accept the views of others. But, in the long run, these unresolved problems may undermine the process of implementing decisions as resentment remains as an undercurrent affecting the relationship.

'Integration' is a third method of resolving conflict and it is the one that Follet recommends. In this method, all the groups involved in the conflict participate fully and freely in discussions relevant to the situation. The participants are allowed to look objectively at the problem without giving any consideration to the position or personality of each person in the process. The most important factor to be considered is the problem at hand. Each person is given the opportunity to make his or her contribution to the discussions and the pros and cons of each suggestion are freely analysed. In the end, the solution to the problem is guided by "the law of the situation".

Follet believed firmly in the importance of cooperative effort in the achievement of organizational goals. She felt that the use of authority as a tool to force subordinates to obey orders was not a good foundation for cooperation. She established clear guidelines for giving orders, and she pointed out that communication was more than 'what' is said. An important aspect of good communication is 'how' it is said.

In her view, coordination was the central role of management. The manager is expected to carry out this role as a continuous process. This has to be done by direct contact with all the participants in the organization. All parts of the organization should work in tandem to achieve the organization's goals.

Mary Parker Follet's work formed a direct bridge between the classical and human relations schools, which developed later. Many of the concepts that are found in the works of the organizational humanists first appeared in papers delivered by Follett at conferences.

Chester Irving Barnard: 1886–1961

Chester Barnard was another theorist whose views fall into this category of neoclassicists and who profoundly influenced the shift of management theory from the more autocratic approaches of the classical theorists. He also believed in the hierarchical structure of formal organizations, but he gained some of his inspiration from other neoclassical theorists. In his notable work, *The Functions of the Executive* (1938), he developed a theory about the power relationship that exists between employers and employees. Barnard built his theory on the view that both employers and employees have some power, that it was not a one-sided situation and that the subordinate had the power to accept or refuse an order given by his superior. He identified what he called the employee's "zone of indifference", a limit beyond which he or she would not go to carry out given orders.

Acceptance Theory of Authority

Bernard's acceptance theory of authority included the bases on which authority is accepted. He emphasized the need for managers to follow these considerations:

- The given order should be understood by the subordinate, otherwise he or she would not be able to carry it out.

- The subordinate should believe that the order is in keeping with the purpose of the organization.

- The order should be considered to be in the interest of the subordinate.

- The subordinate receiving the order should be capable of complying with the order.

A significant part of Barnard's neoclassical approach is the notion of equilibrium. In this approach, he expressed the opinion that management needed to provide an acceptable quality and quantity of incentives to keep the subordinates' contributions to the organization at a high level. In his view, the employees' contributions are maintained in a state of equilibrium or 'steady balance' through the concept of 'contribution-satisfaction'. This suggests that employees will contribute their efforts to the achievement of organizational goals in return for an acceptable amount of satisfaction. Hence, it is the responsibility of the management to ensure that subordinates are induced to cooperate with management and to ensure that efforts to exercise authority take into consideration the fact that the subordinate has the power to influence the success or failure of an organization in achieving its goals.

In Barnard's work, as in others of that era, the individual is given an important place in the production matrix.

George Elton Mayo: 1880–1949

George Elton Mayo, a trained psychologist, was born in Adelaide, Australia, in December 1880. He migrated to the United States in 1922, where he became a professor of industrial research at Harvard Graduate School of Business.

In 1923, he conducted an investigation into the causes of high turnover of workers in a textile mill in Philadelphia. Like researchers of his time, Mayo was preoccupied with the material conditions of the job—time and motion concerns, incentive payments, monitoring, and the absence of interaction between employees. Mayo brought his assumptions as an industrial psychologist to the research and was able to convince the managers at the mill that the introduction of short 'rest pauses' would be beneficial in improving production.

His views on the effect of fatigue and monotony were no different from those of the scientific management theorists. Mayo's classification as a neoclassical theorist rests in the fact that, having joined the team of researchers at the Hawthorne experiments during the period 1927-1932 and later becoming the leading researcher, he had completely changed his views of the worker in the organization. Mayo was later described as the father of the human relations movement, as a result of his published findings.

Summary

Neoclassical theorists made the first attempts at modifying the principles, processes and structures described and prescribed by the earlier theorists. They questioned some of their basic assumptions and developed new approaches to the management of people, the use of authority, the giving of orders and the management of conflict. They, therefore, laid the foundation for the development of other schools of management thought.

References

Barnard, Chester (1938) *The Functions of the Executive* (Harvard University Press, Cambridge, Mass.).

Brown, J.A.C. (1954) "The Social Psychology of Industry", pp. 11-40, in *Historical Retrospect* (Penguin Books, Middlesex, England).

Cole, G.A. (November, 2003) *Management: Theory & Practice,* op cit, pp. 36-39 (Cengage Learning, London).

Follet, Mary Parkes in Luther Galick & Urwick (1937) "The Process of Control", in *Early Sociology of Management and Organizations: Papers on the Science of Administration* (Routledge, London and New York City).

Online Resource

Schwartz, Andrew E. and Dropo, Carla (n.d.) Tools for Becoming a Successful Manager, http://www.allbusiness.com/management/154292-1.html.

The Behavioral School

Introduction

The significance of this discourse is that it represented a major change in the methodologies applied to the study of people in organizations and in the assumptions that had been made about the factors that influenced their behavior. As a result of a series of studies and experiments carried out at the Hawthorne Plant of the Western Electric Company in Chicago between 1924 and 1932 (in which Elton Mayo was involved), the idea of a phenomenon known as 'the Hawthorne effect' has found its way into the theory of organization and management.

From a historical perspective, the studies were carried out in two parts—the early Hawthorne Studies (1924–1927) and the Hawthorne Experiments (1927–1932). The overall result of the studies was that they led to a more humanistic approach to the development of organization theory.

The Hawthorne Studies (1924–1927)

The Hawthorne Studies were carried out by a group of researchers at the above-mentioned Hawthorne Plant. In the mid-1920s, the Hawthorne Plant was the largest factory of the Western Electric Company, which manufactured telephone equipment for Bell Telephone Company, which later became American Telegraph and Telephone Co. (AT&T).

At the time of these studies, the company had some 30,000 employees on its payroll, which was considered large by any standard. Its special feature was the reputation that it had developed for being very progressive in its management practices. The managers had been applying the scientific management principles developed by classical theorists such as Frederick Taylor. These principles include developing the best way of doing a job and finding the best man for the job.

Furthermore, the company was providing very modern welfare benefits for their employees—pension schemes, a sickness benefits scheme, leave with pay and recreational and other facilities. These provisions were not standardized in factory operations at that time.

In the early 1920s, the management was dismayed by the fact that workers were becoming very restive and expressing much dissatisfaction with their working conditions. So these 'progressive' managers decided to seek assistance from the experts in the field of industrial psychology. They called in 'efficiency experts' to research the company's operations and to find out the causes of the dissatisfaction among the workers. Their real concern was the effect that the restiveness was having on production. These experts attempted to solve the problems using the methods that they were trained to believe would solve all industrial problems. These methods included the following:

- Altering the working hours, making them longer or shorter

- Changing the times given for the employees to rest

- Adjusting the lighting in the work area—increasing or decreasing the intensity

During that time, the researchers were focusing on environmental (maintenance) conditions in the workplace but the results were all inconclusive. They were not able to find any relationship between these factors and workers' production.

In spite of these setbacks the managers at the plant persisted with the studies. In 1924, they welcomed a research project promoted by the National Research Council to study the relationship between illumination and individual efficiency. For three years these researchers worked on studying the relationship between the workers' efficiency and lighting in the plant. This study, called the Illumination Experiments, was carried out using a scientific method. Two groups of operators were placed under similar conditions for observation. In one group (the experimental group) the intensity (brightness) of the light was changed upwards and downwards at different periods, while in the other group (the control group) no changes were made to the lighting. Throughout the study it was found that there was a significant increase in the level of production. Even when the light was reduced to very poor levels, the production continued to rise. The fact that production also increased in the group in which there was no change in the lighting led the researchers to conclude that the key to improved production was in some factor other than lighting.

The limitation of the scientific research lay in the fact that it was believed that the worker was an individual unit who could be studied in isolation from other workers. As long as these assumptions about people remained the same, and as long as they continued to look only at physical (environmental) factors, the results would remain inconclusive.

The experiments and the absence of conclusive evidence of the relationship between physical factors and the level of production undermined the theories of the industrial psychologists and others whose theories were based on these assumptions. While it cannot be stated conclusively that environmental factors did not affect production, there was a change in the views about the extent to which these factors had an impact on workers' output.

After three years of studies and experimentation, the decision was taken to change the method of study from the traditional approach, to discard the emphasis on physical factors and to focus the study on human factors. The next phase of the study is referred to as the classical Hawthorne experiments, with which Elton Mayo is associated.

The Hawthorne Experiments (1927–1932)

The name most popularly associated with the Hawthorne Experiments is Elton Mayo (referred to in the neoclassical school), a trained psychologist who had developed a reputation for his work in a textile mill in Philadelphia in 1923. Like researchers of his ilk, he was preoccupied with the material conditions of the job—time and motion concerns, incentive payments, monotony. He was able to convince the managers of the mill that the introduction of short rest pauses and more interaction between employees would help to improve production.

The second stage of the studies at the Hawthorne Plant was conducted; and each phase revealed findings that were precursors to the later development of the human relations school of management thought.

The Relay Assembly Test Room Experiment (1927–1929)

This was the first stage of the experiments in which Mayo was involved. Mayo did not design the studies; in fact he joined the team of researchers a year after the work was in progress. However, on joining the group he established a relationship with the executive of the plant, and subsequently emerged as a natural leader.

The purpose of the study was "to record all the conditions—physiological and social as well as industrial and engineering changes—that might be relevant to workers' performance".

The investigators selected two women who were asked to select four others, making a small group of six women. They were put to work in a small department and their job was to assemble a small but intricate piece of telephone equipment called a relay. They sat on a long bench in assembly line pattern and the finished product was mechanically counted and slipped down a chute.

At the start of the experiments, normal scientific methods were used—recording of the production rate at the start then measuring the changes that resulted when adjustments were made to certain variables. During the experiments, an observer sat with the women in the room and they were also visited by senior company officials and other interested persons. However, no real attempt was made to analyse social relationships. The focus continued to be on changes in physical conditions: rest pauses were introduced, working hours were shortened and lunch times were varied in duration and length. Throughout the time, the women were told what the experimenters were doing and all the time productivity increased, whether conditions were made better or worse. Even when all the special benefits were removed, production continued to increase. In addition to the output in production, there was also an observed change in the women's attitude towards their work. J.A.C. Brown (1970, p.72), quoting from works by Stuart Chase in *The Proper Study of Mankind and Men at Work*, made the following observation:

> "By asking their help and cooperation the investigators had made the girls feel important. Their whole attitude had changed from that of separate cogs in a machine to that of a congenial group trying to help the company solve a problem".

This change in attitude, which caused production to remain positive despite negative changes in working conditions, has come to be known as 'the Hawthorne effect'. The women's response to the interest shown in their work and the group, rather than on the individual was influencing their behavior.

Another challenge to previous ideas about how work should be ordered came out of the group activity. Instead of following the standardized movement of the production line, the women varied the technique in order to avoid monotony. They worked faster and better than ever and this seriously questioned the notion of the 'one best way' of Scientific Management. The women also exercised their own discipline rather than having discipline imposed from above. This also questioned the assumption of administrative and bureaucratic management, which suggested that hierarchical control was the best way to achieve efficiency.

The main conclusions drawn from this stage of the experiments were as follows:

- The group is an important unit in the organization. This challenged the previously held view of man as a purely individualistic being.

- The business (enterprise) performs two major functions:
  – an economic function—producing goods and services
  – a social function—distributing human satisfaction among its employees

- No matter how many systems are put in place to improve efficiency, there will be no significant improvement if the human organization is out of balance.

Following on the conclusions drawn about the effect that people's feelings had on production, the decision was taken to test employees' attitudes throughout the plant. This led to the implementation of the interview programme in 1928.

The Interview Programme (1928–1930)

The objective of this programme was to gather as much information as possible on how workers felt about their working conditions and their jobs. At first, the interviews were structured and did not allow the workers any room for self-expression. They were asked questions such as "Do you like your supervisor?", "Is he fair?" However, the answers were not very helpful in providing reliable information. The employees were promised that their answers would be kept confidential, but that did not help the researchers to get any more than simple 'yes' or 'no' answers.

The interviewers then decided to change the approach to a 'non-directive' method. This meant that the workers were allowed to talk freely while the interviewers listened. The interviewers were counseled not to give advice and not to argue with the respondents. They should remain neutral and treat all information confidentially.

As a result of this programme, the psychological aspects of the behavior of people in an organization were made clearer. It was observed that giving a person the opportunity to speak and to express his or her grievances could help to improve morale. An example was given of a woman who had complained about the poor quality of the food in the canteen. She later thanked the team for their intervention in getting the company to improve the quality of the food. In fact, they had done nothing about her complaint.

A second observation was that people's real concerns were not always about what they expressed aloud, but might be about more deep-seated concerns. A third observation was that the demands that workers made were influenced by situations both inside and outside the factory. For example, matters related to the worker's family could affect his or her feelings while at the workplace. The large amount of information gathered over a two-year period from some 20,000 employees provided a wealth of information from which to conclude that people were not only social beings but there was also a psychological aspect to people at work.

Between 1930 and 1932, there were other modifications to the experiments.

The Bank Wiring Observation Room Experiments (1932)

This represented the final stage of the Hawthorne experiments. After spending nearly five years in the factory, the researchers noticed that social groups tended to develop and that these groups had a strong influence on the behavior of their members. For example, they noticed that there were some restrictions placed on output in some departments and that even the offer of money incentives did not change their action. This attitude was a challenge because it did not fit in with earlier views about money as a motivator. The Bank Wiring Observation Room was set up with 14 men involved in producing equipment called a telephone bank. There were special functions involved in the operation—nine men attached wires to the bank, three soldered them and there were two inspectors. The objective of this observation was different from the previous ones. The researchers were not interested in altering work output, but rather in observing group behavior. The findings from this study were perhaps the most significant and influential of all, and they still continue to influence management today.

The researchers found that the men, working away from the rest of the factory employees, soon developed spontaneously into a team. The team had informal leaders who emerged as the need for a leader arose. The group made decisions about the amount of work that should be done on a daily basis, and these outputs did not coincide with those set by the management. Offers of increased incentives had no effect on the workers' production levels. The men had their own unofficial code of behavior and members were expected to obey them. There was no overproduction ('rate busting') or underproduction ('chiseling'). The group was expected to protect its own interests and not act in any way detrimental to the members.

The conclusions from the Bank Wiring Observation Room Experiments have had a profound influence on the development of organization theory. The study of groups in the organization is a direct result of these studies. The following was concluded from this section of the research:

- No collection of people can be in contact for any length of time without informal groupings arising and natural leaders being pushed to the top.
- It is not only foolish but futile to try to break up these groups.

The Hawthorne research studies ended in 1932; this was assumed to have been related to the Great Depression of the late 1920s and early 1930s. Despite some criticism of the Hawthorne studies, their contribution to the development of management theory is invaluable. The works of Mayo and his associates lay the foundation on which research into human relations theories has been based.

Summary

This study of the various stages of the experiments carried out at the Hawthorne Plant of the General Electric Company represents the first set of scientific research studies into the attitudes and behavior of people at work. Conclusions drawn from the experiments, which lasted five years (1927–1932), moved the development of management theory a step further towards recognizing that people play an important part in the production process.

The research studies, which started out as a study of physiological factors (lighting, rest-pauses, incentive payments), developed to the point where it was recognized that there were also social, psychological and socio-psychological aspects of the human organization. Perhaps the most profound finding was the effect that groups had on production, and the conclusions drawn were that the social side of man was as important as the economic side.

Online Resource

The Hawthorn effect (November 3) In *The Economist* www.economist.com/node/12510632

The Human Relations Theorists

Introduction

This school of management thought has its genesis in the industrial research studies carried out by industrial psychologists in England during World War I (1914–1918). The main focus of these research studies was on such psychological factors as mental and physical fatigue, and on maintenance factors such as lighting and ventilation.

The series of studies carried out at the Hawthorne Plant in Chicago between the mid-1920s and late 1930s stimulated an increase in the number and content of theories on human motivation. These studies helped to change the perception that people who worked in an organization (industry) were purely 'economic beings' whose main interest was in material gain. The shift was towards seeing people also as 'social beings'.

The conclusions drawn from these studies did not, however, provide all the answers to questions about why people work. This has been the major focus of the human relations theorists, who also have been referred to as motivation theorists.

They also have been concerned to find out the reasons for differences in performance between groups of persons doing the same work. Several observations have been made and answers given to this phenomenon, which include the following:

- Differences in abilities or skills of individual workers

- Different amounts and kinds of experiences

- Differences in the degree to which the individual possesses the necessary intellectual capacity to learn from these experiences

On the basis of these assumptions, managers have used several kinds of strategies to improve workers' performance. For example:

- They have made special efforts to employ workers with the abilities and skills to do a particular job. This approach is similar to that put forward by
  – scientific management theory (ie, finding the best man for the job) and

29

> – the bureaucratic principle – "officials should be selected on the basis of technical competence".

- They have placed emphasis on
  – systematic on-the-job training (recommended by Taylor) and
  – changes in the content of the job to match the ability and skill of the worker.

One of the assumptions about the cause of these differences in worker performance, which had yet to be included in the work output equation, was the difference in motivation. In addressing the challenges of this area of study, one theorist expressed the opinion that

> "The psychology of motivation is tremendously complex, and what has been unraveled with any degree of assurance is small indeed. But the dismal ratio of knowledge to specialization has not dampened the enthusiasm for new forms of snake oil that are constantly coming on the market many of them with academic testimonials" (Herzberg, 1968).

This text has selected for special consideration by a small group of human relations theorists from the vast amount of literature produced from this theoretical perspective.

Abraham Maslow: Hierarchy of Needs

Abraham Maslow, an American social psychologist, was one of the earliest theorists to study human motivation. His theory of the hierarchy of needs is perhaps the most well-known of all the motivational theories, and his views greatly influenced the other theorists in the school. His theory was based on the belief that the human being was a 'wanting animal'. In essence, this means that people have needs that constantly have to be satisfied. These needs, however, do not appear in a random, erratic way. They are arranged in an orderly way in a kind of hierarchy referred to as an 'order of prepotency'. He theorized that, as soon as one need is satisfied, a stronger need will take its place. He identified this hierarchy of needs in a diagrammatic way as shown below:

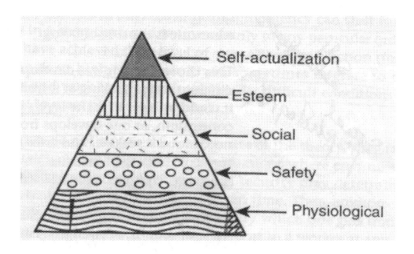

At the lowest level are the 'physiological needs'. These are present at birth, as the child draws his or her first breath. The need for air, food, warmth and sleep are all physiological.

Everyone, according to Maslow, is motivated to seek satisfaction of these needs and will engage in actions that lead to this end. These physiological needs cannot be satisfied once and for all. They can only be relatively satisfied. For example, the need for food can only be satisfied as long as it takes the digestive system to process what one eats, then one is hungry again. But when the need is relatively satisfied (and this can mean that even if the need cannot be immediately satisfied, knowledge of the possibility of satisfaction in the near future will be sufficient), then another need will take its place or become 'prepotent'.

According to Maslow, the second level of need is for safety or security. At this level, there is the need for protection, to have some sense that one can expect to be free from danger in relationships with others and in the environment in general. Once safety and security needs are relatively satisfied, the next higher level of need is the 'belonging need', or the need for social interaction. People develop a desire to be part of a group, to relate and cooperate with others, to give and receive affection.

As Maslow theorized, the needs will continue to ascend up the hierarchy and as soon as a person feels content with those around him or her, that person will not be satisfied to be just a part of the pack. The need to be recognized, to be 'esteemed' by others, will emerge. Here, the ego takes over and the individual wants to have status in the group, separate from group association—to have self-respect and have the respect of others.

The highest level of need in the hierarchy is the 'self-fulfillment or self-actualization need'. This, in essence, means that one wants to be, in the final analysis, what one is capable of being.

Critique of Maslow's Theory

Although Maslow's theory of human motivation was developed from the perspective of a social psychologist, it has been widely accepted and integrated into management theory. However, several questions have been raised about its applicability to the management of large-scale organizations that employ a variety of individuals with differences in their levels of needs in the hierarchy or their position on the continuum of psychological development.

There are questions about the role of culture or personality trait in the development of the needs hierarchy. The problem for managers, therefore, is how to develop a uniform standard for motivating individuals, bearing in mind the random state of needs among employees.

While these arguments do not negate the basic tenets of the theory, they raise questions about its relevance to managers in organizations where environmental factors, socialization or levels of personal security may determine which need is prepotent in an employee at any given time. Thus, environmental factors, socialization or the amount of security that one gets from other sources might determine which need is prepotent in a worker at any given time.

Douglas McGregor: Theory X v. Theory Y

The work of Douglas McGregor, as it relates to the theory of human motivation, is perhaps the most misinterpreted of the motivation theorists. It must be clarified that McGregor is not a proponent of the assumptions of the Theory X theory of motivation. He began his development of a theory of human motivation by first describing and, in essence, criticizing the assumptions of traditional managers and the conventional wisdom that they hold about people in organizations.

Douglas McGregor developed a theory of human motivation by first describing the conventional (traditional) views that managers hold about people. These views, which he referred to as 'assumptions', are said to be found in all the current literature on organizations and on managerial policy and practices. He pointed out that all managerial decisions are based on these assumptions about human nature and human behavior. The conventional assumptions that he labeled Theory X include the following views:

Theory X

- It is the responsibility of managers to direct the efforts of employees, as well as to organize the other elements of production—money, material and equipment—in the interest of the achievement of the organization's economic functions.

- Managers must design strategies to "get things done through people"; for example, they must coerce them, control their actions and modify their behavior to fit in with the needs of the organization.

- The active intervention of the manager is necessary to prevent the workers from being passive or even resistant to the needs of the organization. Therefore, they must be persuaded, rewarded or punished, directed and controlled.

The strategies of the traditional manager are based on these widespread beliefs about the nature of mankind:

The average person

- has a natural dislike of work and will avoid it as much as possible,

- lacks ambition, dislikes responsibility and prefers to be led,

- is only concerned with his or her own self-interest and not with the needs of the organization,

- is naturally resistant to change, and

- is very easily led astray, not very bright and is impressed by unscrupulous persons

McGregor emphasized that conventional organizations are structured to reflect these assumptions and so are all their managerial policies, practices and programmes. In managing people under these assumptions, managers use the following strategies:

- The 'hard' or 'strong' approach—the manager uses coercion, threat, close supervision and tight control over people

- The 'soft' or 'weak' approach—giving in to workers' demands and being permissive in an effort to achieve harmony

Both extreme approaches have their own set of difficulties. The 'hard' approach can create antagonism among workers and workers can become militant, using counterforce against coercive force and generally restricting output. The 'soft' approach usually leads to a weakening of management. Workers become indifferent, demanding more and more freedom and giving less and less in return. The development of the 'fair but firm' concept is equally ineffective because it combines both the hard and soft approach, but is also based on Theory X assumptions.

McGregor asserted that Theory X assumptions do provide some explanations about human behavior, but these can only be partial. He argued that the negative aspects of people's behavior in organizations are not a consequence of man's inherent nature but of the nature of industrial organizations and the philosophy, policies and practice of management in these organizations. McGregor claims to have drawn his conclusion from the work of Abraham Maslow, a colleague who developed the theory of the 'hierarchy of needs', as previously presented.

In applying Maslow's theory to motivation in organizations, McGregor recognized that management often concentrates on providing only the basic needs satisfaction among its employees—the physiological and safety needs. The traditional manager cannot understand why good wages, good working conditions and excellent fringe benefits do not lead to more production. However, as Maslow theorized, "a satisfied need is not a motivator"; this means that the higher-level motivational needs, such as social, ego or self-actualization needs, are not being addressed. McGregor pointed out that the insistence by people on getting more money is often the result of the lack of satisfaction of these higher-level needs. The indolence, passive attitude, lack of a sense of responsibility and other negative behaviors all result from management's 'hard' or 'soft' approach, which do not stimulate motivation.

Theory Y

McGregor suggested a different approach to management and motivation. He suggested a new set of assumptions about people, which he called Theory Y. Broadly speaking, the theory states the following:

- Management has the responsibility for organizing people and the other elements—money, material, equipment—in the interest of economic ends.

- People are not, by nature, passive and resistant to organizational needs. They have become so as a result of their experience in the organization.

- People in organizations have the motivation, the potential for development and the capacity to assume responsibility. They are ready to direct their behavior to organizational goals and will do so if management makes it possible for them to recognize and develop these human characteristics.

- It is the essential task of management to create the conditions to make it possible for employees to achieve their own goals, as well as the goals of the organization.

McGregor's new theory literally turns around the views of traditional managers, particularly their view on how people should be managed. He said the following:

- Threat of punishment, external control, coercion, etc., are not the only means of motivating people at work.

- Appealing to higher-level needs, such as socializing, esteem and self-actualization, can bring out higher levels of response and participation.

- If the proper conditions are provided, people will not only accept responsibility, they will even seek responsibility.

- A significant number of people in organizations have the capacity to be imaginative, to be creative and to be ingenious.

McGregor suggested that if managers accept these assumptions a wide range of managerial possibilities could be opened, leading to new approaches to management. The new process would involve 'management by objectives', a concept proposed by Peter Drucker, a management expert, who stated that this would be the opposite of 'management by control'. In management by objectives, which is consistent with the Theory Y approach, the following innovative strategies could be employed:

Decentralization and Delegation
In this approach, employees are freed from the too-close supervision and control of the conventional approach. They are allowed to direct their own activities to assume some responsibility. By doing this, each employee gets an opportunity to satisfy ego needs. When the manager delegates, he or she is expressing confidence in the employee and is also freed from some of the day-to-day management functions.

Job Enlargement
This is another approach that is consistent with the assumptions of Theory Y. Job enlargement is not a question of giving the employee more of the same job. This could by very frustrating. The concept is interpreted to mean 'job enrichment', in which case more challenging elements are added to the base task. This encourages employees at the lower levels of the organization to accept responsibility, learn to interact with others at different levels and thus satisfy social and ego needs.

Participative and Consultative Management
This is an approach that, if used under proper conditions, can encourage employees to direct their energies towards achievement of organizational goals. By allowing them to participate in decision-making they get an opportunity to demonstrate their creativity. They are, therefore, able to satisfy their social and ego needs.

However, this approach should be used in a genuine way and not as a farce. The employees should be able to see how their ideas have been applied after they have been accepted by management.

Performance Appraisal
An innovative aspect of 'management by objectives' is the idea that those employees who are allowed to participate in setting the 'targets' or the 'objectives' that they should achieve could also appraise their own performance. By so doing, the employee can measure his or her own output at regular intervals and, where necessary, and take steps to correct deficiencies. By committing to a goal, the individual can be self-motivated and ego needs can be satisfied.

These views on human motivation were first presented by McGregor in the late 1950s. He then expressed the view that the process of releasing the human potential through a new approach to management would be slow, costly and sometimes discouraging. Notwithstanding the challenges, he was of the view that if the ideas were applied to the "human side of enterprise" they could enhance the materialistic achievements that were made in the previous decades.

Frederick Herzberg's Hygiene-Motivation Theory

Another theorist in the early group of human relationists is Frederick Herzberg. He readily acknowledged the problems that are associated with the development of a theory of motivation by stating the following:

> "This psychology of motivation is tremendously complex, and what has been unraveled with any degree of assurance is small indeed. But the dismal ratio of knowledge to speculation has not dampened the enthusiasm for new forms of snake oil that are constantly coming on the market, many of them with academic testimonials" (Herzberg, 1968).

Herzberg derived his theory of motivation first from research that he and a group of associates carried out among some 200 engineers and accountants in a cross-section of industry in Pittsburgh, Pennsylvania.

The study was designed to test the concept that people have two distinctly different sets of needs. The first set of needs was called 'animal needs', and these were the in-built needs that everyone has to avoid pain. These needs are physiological, such as the need to satisfy hunger. From these needs would arise the necessity to earn money, which then becomes a drive or motivation. The second set of needs is 'human needs'. These are related to the psychological features of human characteristics, which include the need to grow, to achieve and to actualize (to become).

In the study, the respondents were asked to identify events in their work experience that either gave them marked improvement in job satisfaction or reduced their job satisfaction. The findings from this study indicated that the factors in the work situation that produced job satisfaction (and motivation) were different from those that led to job dissatisfaction. The first set of factors, that is, those that were strong determinants of job satisfaction, were identified as follows:

- Achievement—getting results from efforts
- Recognition —being regarded for input in work
- The work itself—work being a vocation or calling
- Responsibility—enrichment of the job
- Advancement—moving ahead in the job situation

Herzberg called these factors 'satisfiers'.

On the other side of the work situation, there were some factors that, although they did not lead to positive job attitudes or job satisfaction, served to prevent dissatisfaction. These were referred to as 'dissatisfiers'. The most prominent ones that showed up in the survey were as follows:

- Company policy and administration
- Supervision

- Salary

- Interpersonal relations

- Working conditions

The first group of factors are said to be 'motivators' and the second set are called 'hygiene' factors. The distinction between the two sets of factors can be found in what a person does and the conditions under which it is done. Here are some qualities or properties of a motivator:

- It is intrinsic to the job—it is related to the job content

- It satisfies human needs—social, ego, esteem, actualization

- It is not the opposite of a dissatisfier because it is not in the same category.

On the other hand, dissatisfiers are factors that are outside the content of the job, or they are extrinsic to the job. They are important to the worker because they are necessary for maintenance, just as air, water, warmth and light. But they do not cause the employee to have job satisfaction.

The hygiene-motivation theory says that additional increases in the intrinsic factors such as

- the quality of work content,

- the possibility for advancement on the job,

- recognition by superiors for work well done, and

- additional responsibility based on additional capability

will lead to more job satisfaction. On the other hand, increases in the extrinsic factors, also called the 'job context', will decrease the dissatisfaction, but will not increase job satisfaction.

For example, it is argued that a salary increase can provide a good feeling for a time, but if the job is boring and offers no scope for advancement it will lead to a loss of interest, and the employee will not be motivated.

On a personal level, if a supervisor is friendly, asks regularly about workers' feelings and makes sure that working conditions are good, this will not help motivation. Similarly, if the supervisor gives the subordinate only routine tasks that do not provide any opportunity to apply his or her skills, these stimuli may give some short-term satisfaction but their ability to be motivators will be short-lived.

Herzberg developed a thesis on management and motivation in which he criticized some of the 'carrot and stick' approaches that managers used in their attempt to motivate workers. Those approaches, which are obviously negative, are the 'stick' and include physical force and psychological attacks (eg, insults, bawling out). The intention is to get the employee to perform, but instead he or she feels resentment and often reacts negatively. Those acts which fall in the category of 'carrot' appear to be positive but they are also considered 'dissatisfiers' (ie, maintenance or hygiene factors) include rewards, incentives, even increased status. In Herzberg's view, these things give employees a jump start, but they are not motivators. He uses an analogy by making reference to the way you get a dog to move—a kick from the rear is a negative force that can get a short-term result. A dog biscuit in front of his nose is frontal force; it can result in movement but it is not motivation because the stimulus is from outside.

Herzberg makes the point that the difference between the hygiene factors (whether negative or positive) and real motivators is like the difference between giving the individual a jump start or recharging his or her battery by outside stimulation and the individual having his or her own internal generator.

Other Human Relations Theorists

In addition to the three well-known theorists discussed above, there are some others who have written on the problems of human motivation in organizations. Although they have not seriously challenged the views of the earlier theorists, they have added some new dimensions to the understanding of the behavior in organizations. Following are the views of some of these theorists.

Rensis Likert

Rensis Likert's contribution to the concept of motivation centres on his theory of 'high-producing managers'. Here, the focus is on managers and supervisors who were able to achieve the highest levels of productivity with the lowest cost and the highest levels of employee motivation.

Likert's observation was made from research carried out in industrial and governmental organizations in the United States. He found that, in organizations in which performance was at a consistently high standard, there was a sense of personal worth and importance that was gained from belonging to a work group. He observed that the aspirations of the employees were realized through the 'participative management approach' employed by managers. The research also revealed that the highest levels of employee motivation and satisfaction were found where managers were employing management principles and practices that deviated from the traditional approaches and general practices that were prescribed by the classical theorists.

Chris Argyris

Chris Argyris's motivation theory was centred on the relationship between the needs of people and the needs of the organization. He developed the 'immaturity-maturity theory' to explain the apathetic and otherwise negative behavior of employees in organizations.

The framework of ideas developed by Argyris was based in the assumption that human beings tend to develop from infants to adults along a continuum of psychological growth, which includes development from

- a state of being passive to a state of being increasingly active,
- a state of dependence on others to a state of relative independence,
- a subordinate position in a family and society to aspiring to an equal or superordinate position relative to peers; and
- a lack of awareness of self to an awareness of and control over self

Following on these assumptions, Argyris concluded that most of the human problems in organizations arise because relatively healthy people are asked to participate in work situations that force them to be dependent, subordinate and submissive and to use only a few of their more developed abilities. He posited the view that the structure of the formal organization, the directive leadership styles and the many managerial controls (eg, budgets, incentives, quality control) are variables that cause employee dependence. In his view, the degree of subordination caused by these variables tends to increase as one goes down the chain of command and as the organization takes on the characteristics of mass production.

All these factors are frustrating to healthy human beings, who will respond and adapt to their frustration and the conflicts that arise by using any one or combination of the following informal activities:

- Leave the situation

- Become defensive

- Become apathetic, disinterested in the organization and its formal goals

- Create informal groups to defend themselves against reaction to their behavior

- Formalize their group into trade unions

- Place less emphasis on self-growth, creativity and so on, and emphasize the importance of money and other rewards.

In turn, management will tend to view informal activities as detrimental to the formal organization, which only increases sanctions against employees, which in turn increases employees' informal activities.

Scientific tests of the assumptions of Argyris's theory led to the conclusion that employees modified the organization by creating an informal employee culture that sanctions behavior and helps the employee top self-actualize. According to this theory, it is employees and not management who provide the greater opportunity for them to express a more mature disposition and to move away from the 'infant' end of the personality model.

Victor Vroom developed an 'expectancy theory', which states that human effort is in direct relationship to the expected satisfaction of their preferences, which are based on their social values. In other words, people make conscious decisions to act in anticipation of the rewards they expect. This theory poses a problem for managers to become more aware of the individual's expectations, the preferences (valence) and his or her willingness to integrate the concept into a given work situation.

David McLelland's motivation theory examines the incentives that guide the individual's action. He identified three basic needs: achievement, application and power.

He stated that individuals motivated by achievement are driven by the need to improve an existing condition and will formulate ideas, take action and even take the necessary risk to bring about that change.

Affiliation-oriented individuals are more focused on family and friends and will be less driven by productivity goals than achievement-oriented individuals. A gender analysis has been applied to this need as it has been stated that women have a greater need for affiliation, although a cultural perspective could also be taken in such analysis.

Individuals who are motivated by power are those who associate specific action with the power to be gained from that action. The need to get recognition, command attention and gain control is generally prepotent in these individuals. The theorist also recommended that managers should identify the differential need of the employees and develop motivational strategies to meet those needs.

Summary

Theories of human motivation run along a continuum of needs from physical to psychological, sociological and psycho-social. It must be noted that these theories were developed in different economic, social, and cultural environments. Consequently, while they provide some basis for understanding the behavior of people in organizations they do not fully explain the behavior of individuals in diverse environmental situations, in both developed and developing states.

References

Argyris, Chris (1983) "Action Science and Intervention", in *Journal of Applied Behavioural Science,* vol. 19, pp. 115-40.

Brown, T.A.C. (1970) "The Work of Elton Mayo", in *The Social Psychology of Industry,* pp. 69-96, (Penguin Books, Middlesex, England).

Cole, G.A. (1990) "Major Theories of Human Motivation", in *Management Theory and Practice,* ELRS 3rd ed., pp. 40-66 (D P Publications, London).

Herzberg, Frederick (1959) *The Motivation to Work,* 2nd ed., op cit, pp. 86-90 (John Wiley & Sons, New York)

Herzberg, Frederick (1968) "One More Time, How Do You Motivate Employees", *Harvard Business Review*, vol. 46, pp. 53-62.

Likert, Rensis (1961) *New Patterns of Management,* pp. 97-104 (McGraw Hill Companies, New York).

Maslow, A.H (1992) "A Theory of human motivation", *Psychological Review,* vol. 50, pp. 370-96

Mayo, Elton (1949) *The Social Problems of an Industrial Civilization* (Cap. 4) (Roalledge, London).

McGregor, Douglas (1960) *The Human Side of Enterprise,* (McGraw Hill Book Co., New York).

Roethlisberger F.J. and Dickson, F.W. (1939) *Management and the Worker.* (Harvard University Press, Cambridge, Mass.).

Vroom, Victor and Deci, Edward L. (1943) *Management and Motivation,* pp. 39-51 (Penguin Books, London).

Online Resources

Maslow, Abraham H. (1943) Theories of Human Motivation, Andrew Maslow, http://www.google.com/search?q=theories+of+human+motivation&rls=com. microsoft:en-us&ie=UTF-8&oe=UTF-8&startIndex=&startPage=1

Motivating Employees. Inc. magazine, http://www.inc.com/guides/hr/20776.html

Management by Objectives (MBO) Motivating people by aligning their objectives with the goals of the organization, http://www.mindtools.com/pages/article/newTMM_94.htm

What Do Managers Do, The Wall Street Journal, How-To Guide, http://guides.wsj.com/management/developing-a-leadership-style/what-do-managers-do/

Decision-Making Theories

Introduction

Although the classical theorists did not develop a theory of decision-making, close scrutiny of their views will reveal that they integrated the need for a more 'rational' approach to the management processes—planning, organizing, directing and controlling. By the mid-20th century, however, the idea of a theory of decision-making had emerged mainly because of the work of Herbert Simon, who identified a relationship between decision-making and organizations. It was his view that instead of just focusing on structures, processes or even on people to find the answer to organizational efficiency, it is also important to examine the decision-making process.

According to Simon, the organization is a complex system in which decisions are made at every point, and all members of the organization are decision-makers. Consequently, each individual has the capacity to influence the outcome of decisions made within the organizational context. These views have some commonality with those of neoclassicists, including Chester Barnard, who earlier developed the "acceptance theory of authority", and Mary Parker Follet, who expressed the view that individuals in the organization have the power to undermine the process of implementation of decisions with which they were not in agreement and are, therefore, decision-makers themselves.

Several theorists contend for priority of place in the development of decision-making theories. It has been observed that the development of new theories has followed a pattern in which existing theories have been criticized and an attempt made to replace them with one that most closely resembles the real situation. It then becomes evident that the value-framework of these theorists forms an important part of their theoretical construct.

Models of Decision-Making

In spite of these theoretical issues, it follows that each individual is a decision-maker and that each individual should develop capability and skills in decision-making.

While all decision-makers consciously or unconsciously use a style or pattern or model of decision-making, it is important that all participants in the organization seek to make decisions that follow the management principle of 'unity of direction'. In theories of decision-making, a number of models have been identified, analysed and criticized. They fall along a continuum from the 'rational comprehensive' to the 'extra-rational' approach.

The Rational Comprehensive Model

This ideal decision-making model is based on the classical economic theory, which assumes that the decision-maker goes through a comprehensive process of information-gathering and data analysis to arrive at an optimum decision, one that will give the decision-maker the highest net benefit. Charles Lindblom, a political scientist at Yale University, described this analytical method as follows:

- The decision-maker is faced with a specific problem that can be isolated from other problems.

- The goals or values are selected and ranked according to their importance.

- All possible approaches for achieving the goals or values are known.

- The consequences and costs of each alternative approach can be predicted.

- The consequences of any approach can be compared with those of all other alternatives.

- The decision-maker then chooses the alternatives that have consequences most clearly matching the predetermined goals.

The goal of this method is to arrive at a rational decision through a method of scientific investigation and scientific problem-solving. The model is built on a process in which analysts define the problem, develop alternatives, place values on the consequences of the alternatives, assess probability that it will occur and make choices based on the logical assumption that the decision will yield the highest net satisfaction.

The Satisfying Model

Herbert Simon, who in the 1990s made the connection between decision-making and organizations, recognized that the actual behavior falls short of objective rationality and proposed a principle of 'bounded rationality'. In this behavior-alternative model, Simon argues that while 'economic man' can deal with the real world because he possesses all relevant knowledge, 'administrative man' is satisfied with less information and analysis than the rational comprehensive model suggests. Simon's theory of 'intended' or 'bounded' rationality refers to administrative behavior that 'satisfies' rather than 'maximizes'. One of the fundamental characteristics of this model is that "choice in administration is always exercised with respect to a limited appropriate simplified model of the real situation".

Simon's main thesis is that "the central concern of administrative theory is with the boundary between the rational and nonrational aspects of human social behavior".

Simon, who was a strong advocate of management science for achieving satisfactory standards of decision-making, coined the term 'satisfying', a combination of 'satisfy' and 'suffice', but this theory was not without criticism from other theorists. Hence, the difference between the comprehensively rational decision and 'bounded rationality' is the difference between "searching for a needle in a haystack and searching for a needle which is sharp enough to sew with".

The Incrementalist Model

Charles Lindblom, whose concern was mainly with decision-making in the arena of public policy-making, argued that the 'idealized' theory of decision-making needed to be revised. He subsequently proposed an alternative approach to decision-making, which goes beyond Simon's view by emphasizing the all-pervasive significance of limitations in human and organizational decision-making. Instead of the rational approach to decision-making, he suggests the method of 'successive limited comparisons', by which the administrator considers only a limited set of policy alternatives that are incremental additions or modifications of a broader set of policies.

Lindblom argued that complex public policy problems could not be solved through a rational-comprehensive approach, because of the possibility of conflict between interested and contending parties, and given the limitations of human capability and constraints of time and material resources.

The incremental approach is a practical method of decision-making that uses the process of 'partisan mutual adjustments' and considers only those values of social objectives on which the decision-makers are agreed. In this model, the measure of a 'good' decision is the degree to which decision-makers are in agreement, while a 'poor' decision ignores participants capable of influencing the projected course of action.

The main criticism of this approach is that it subscribes to the pluralist theory and conveniently gives ideological support to the maintenance of the status quo.

The Mixed Scanning Approach

While agreeing with Lindlomb's attack on the rational approach, which relies on greater resources than the decision-maker commands, Amital Etzioni also identifies serious flaws in the incremental model. His major criticisms are that in the incremental decision-making approach, the following takes place:

- The interests of the most powerful organized partisans will probably get the greater part of the decision-maker's attention.
- Basic social innovations are not encouraged.
- The incremental approach does not apply to fundamental decisions (such as the declaration of war).

Etzioni, therefore, proposed a model that represents a compromise between two, which he calls 'mixed scanning'. This approach is a middle way between pure economic rationality and pure political rationality. He suggests the employment of a technique that is analogous to a weather observation system, employing twin cameras. One camera surveys the whole sky on a regular basis, collecting as much information as possible without going into details and avoiding costly analysis. The other camera focuses on areas needing in-depth study and, applying the incrementalist approach, the manager focuses on those areas in which the decision-makers combine high order fundamental policy-making, which sets basic directions, with a more in-depth examination of those areas in which "similar patterns had developed in the recent past, in perhaps a few nearby regions".

In this 'mixed scorning' strategy the manager is able to include features of both the rationalism and the incrementalism. This approach removes the limitations of using any one model of decision- or policy-making and, rather, accommodates the two extremes in which there is rigorous analysis of available information with quantitative partisan mutual adjustment, which is a requirement in government/political decision-making.

The Extra-Rational Model

Another approach to policy-making, which is presented as being at the opposite end of the continuum from pure rationality, is the 'extra-rational' model. In contrast to the phrasal or linear structure of decision-making proposed by most 'rational' theorists, this decision-making process is nonlinear, but rather "consists of a continuous reaction of what is decided, both on the decision-maker and on the context in which the decision takes place."

The extra-rational theory was elaborated on by Sir Geoffrey Vickers, who soundly rejects rational and incrementalist theories and substituted it with the concept of 'appreciation'. He argues against the nature of pure rationality in decision-making by starting with the view that decision-making is nonlinear and that the direction of a decision is not a ceaseless flow along a continuum.

Appreciation, on the other hand, does not give regard to objective facts because, what appears as facts is usually subjected to individual interpretation. However, appreciation, though 'non-rational' does not suggest inaction on the part of the decision-maker (as administrator).

In his view, decision-making consists of a continuous reaction to what is decided, both on the decision-maker and on the context in which the decision is made. Sir Geoffrey elaborates his position on his nonmechanical and noncausal approach by stating that

> "In institutional behavior the concepts of what ought to be regarded as regulatable, the standards by which they should be regulated, the ways of reconciling the inconsistent demands which they generate, are neither constant nor given, but are themselves a function of the process which they are supposed to govern".

Summary and Conclusions

Decision-making theorists have developed their views from different perspectives— economic, political and social. It has been observed that the theories discussed range along a continuum from the 'purely rational' to the 'extra-rational'. Over time, the development of new theories has followed a pattern in which an existing theory has been criticized and an attempt made to replace it with one that is considered more appropriate. It is clear, however, that the value-framework of the theorists form an important part of their theoretical construct.

The reality that managers face a wide range of decision problems, in different states of nature, makes it impossible for any model to be universally applicable. Different environments—political, economic, social—impinge on the decisional inputs (demands) and outputs, and on their acceptability to their constituents.

The introduction of quantitative technologies has gone a far way towards solving some of the issues and problems associated with the selection of models of decision-making. However, the ubiquity of the need to make decisions within the limits of various time frames, resources and human capacity, makes it clear that nonrational criteria will be an important element in the process of decision-making and 'judgement' and 'intuition' will, consequently, play an important role in the process of decision-making.

References

Barnard, C.I. (1938) *The Functions of the Executive* (Harvard University Press, Cambridge, Mass.)

Boss, R. Wayne (1976) "Decision-Making: Theories and Applications to the Budgetary Process", in R.T. Golembiewiski, F, Gibson, F. Cornag & G.Y. Cornag eds., *Public Administration*, 3rd ed. (Rand McNally College Publishing Co., Chicago).

Etzioni, Amitai (Dec 1976) "Mixed Scanning: A Third Approach to Decision-Making", *Public Administration Review* #27 (ASPA, Washington, DC).

Gulick, Luther and Vrwick L. eds. (1937) *Papers on the Science of Administration* (Institute of Public Administration, New York).

Lindblom, Charles (Dec. 1967) "The Science of Muddling Through", *Public Administration Review,* #27 (ASPA, Washington, DC).

Simon, Herbert (1976) "Decision-Making and Administration Behaviour", in *Administrative Behaviour,* (Collier McMillan Publishers, London).

Spiers, Maurice (1975) *Techniques and Public Administration* (Fontana/Collins, London).

Online Resource

Baldoni, John. (June, 2010) The Five Attributes of Authority, http://www.amanet.org/training/articles/The-Five-Attributes-of-Authority.aspx.

12Manage: The Executive Fast Track, Decision Making and Valuation: Methods, Models and Theories, http://www.12manage.com/i_dv.html.

Systems and Contingency Theory

Introduction

One of the findings from researchers into the behavior of people in organizations is the complexity of the social systems and the interdependence between the variables that comprise organizations as a system.

The studies carried out in the 1940s by the Tavistock Institute at a Welsh coal mine in Great Britain pioneered the development of systems thinking as it applies to an organization. In particular, the studies by Eric Trist, a social psychologist, in collaboration with K.W. Bamforth, an ex-miner, observed the social and psychological problems raised by the introduction of new technology. The researchers were interested in the effects of mechanization on the social and work organization in the 'coal face' (ie, 'coal getting'). The pre-mechanized structure consisted of small, closely knit teams that were responsible for all aspects of the process of extraction. These autonomous groups worked in isolation from other similar groups and formed bonds that also had importance outside the work environment.

The introduction of a mechanized system (the 'longwall' method) led to complete change in the social structure. The small autonomous groups were replaced by shifts of teams with high degrees of task specialization in each activity—cutting coal, shoveling it into conveyors and transporting the coal along the seam.

This breakdown of the closely knit small group had some negative consequences. It resulted in conflicts and competition between the shifts for 'best jobs', rate of pay, blame-passing and an increase in absenteeism. Consequently, the benefits of technical changes were being undermined by changes in the social structure.

The eventual solution to these problems was the introduction of a new system called 'the composite longwall method', which was designed to meet the social needs of miners as well as the economic requirements of management. A new working arrangement was made for all basic operations to be carried out by any one shift, and these tasks were allocated by members of the group. There was also a change in the payment system, to include a group bonus. The introduction of the composite method resulted in increased productivity, reduced absenteeism and lower accident rate.

This research led to the development of the concepts of working groups neither as technical systems nor social systems but as 'interdependent socio-technical systems'. From this perspective, they developed the view that any production system requires both a 'technological organization' (ie, the equipment and process layout) and a 'work organization' (ie, those that carry out the necessary task for each other). Whereas technological factors limit the kind of work organization possible, a work organization has social and psychological properties of its own that are independent of the technology. The socio-technical system is seen not as a closed physical system but as an open living system.

The Systems Approach

The systems approach to management is a modern way of viewing the management of organizations, which was preceded by the classical or mechanistic and, later, the human relations or behavioral approaches. However, this new approach does not eliminate the previous ones; rather, it provides a basis for the integration of all the other theories studied so far. The difference between this modern approach and the earlier ones is that, while earlier theories have been classified as 'partial' in their views, the systems approach is said to be 'wholistic'.

In contrast with the systems approach, the major philosophies of the earlier schools of management thought had the following focus:

In the Classical Schools:

- **Scientific management** focused on the techniques of tasks, and placed the emphasis on finding 'the one best way' of doing a job.

- **Administrative management** focused mainly on the process of managing people and things. The theorists were interested in developing general principles to guide managers in their effort to achieve efficiency and effectiveness.

- **Bureaucratic management** emphasized the importance of the structure of organizations. The characteristics of the bureaucracy included

    · the importance of the hierarchical structure,

    · the notion that employees should be appointed on the basis of their qualification or technical competence, and

    · the importance of having rules and regulations to control the actions of persons in an organization

The human relations school of management shifted the focus from the 'mechanistic' to the 'humanistic' approach to the management of organizations. These theorists were mainly concerned with human needs and how those needs affected the attitude and behavior of people in the organization.

In these approaches, which are referred to as 'closed systems approaches', it is assumed that all the problems that a manager faces can be solved within the structure of the organization.

The Neoclassical theorists, such as Mary Parker Follet, Chester Barnard et al., challenged some of the traditional views and opened the way to a more modern or 'open systems' approach to management, but some of the fundamental principles of 'management by control' were retained in these views.

The Concept of Systems

A system is defined as a collection of "mutually interdependent parts of an element". This means that each part is dependent for its functioning on the proper functioning of all the other parts. Systems theory also holds the view that the organization as a system interacts with an external environment with which it also has an interdependent relationship. The theory borrows ideas from the physical, biological and social sciences.

Systems theory treats organizations, whether industrial, commercial, government, academic or social, as living organisms. Like an organism, an organization can be created, grow from small beginnings to maturity or wither and die. It can split into separate parts, each with a life of its own, or it can merge with others to become an organism of a higher order. Some systems have a short life, while others endure, adapting to changes in their environment or resisting change until they become outdated within their environment.

The organization as a system has its own internal set of mutually independent parts, such as machines, workers, raw materials, goods and services, sales personnel and management. If the organization is to function efficiently and effectively, all these elements must work in unison. Workers cannot work without appropriate technology—machines or raw material. Sales personnel need goods and services to be sold, and the organization would have no direction without management to plan the activities, organize the human and material resources, direct the action of employees or evaluate the result of a plan of action. The processes in the system move in a circular manner in which all the elements are dependent on the others. All the parts of the organization as a system have an interdependent relationship with each other.

Applying Systems Thinking to Management

Systems thinking is important to understanding and practising management. Although the organization is recognized as a system, the manager who is practicing systems thinking will see the problem through critical lenses. He or she will realize that

- what is done in one part of the organization will affect the other parts,

- what occurs in one system will not only affect the other parts of that particular system but will affect other systems as well, and

- the effects or consequences of action in any element of the system cannot be predicted definitively—some results are unintentional consequences; and the solution of any one problem may produce or create one or more new problems.

The External Environment

In order to effectively apply the systems approach, a manager has to be aware of the three important characteristics in the relationship between the organization and its external environment. These are as follows:

1. The organization receives input from the environment, which include demands, resources, material and human financial information and values.

2. The input demands are categorized, organized, acted on and transformed into goods and services.

3. The finished products are exported into the external environment.

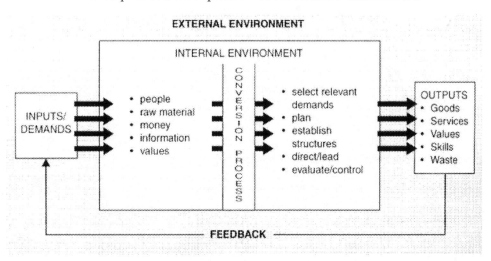

The organization as an open system maintains its equilibrium (or balance) through a dynamic process in which it exchanges outputs with its external environment and receives feedback (either negative or positive) from that environment. The informational feedback then becomes another input into the system.

The Internal Environment

The internal network of subsystems in the organization also keeps the organization in equilibrium. One writer identified five subsystems that are relevant to the process. They are as follows:

The goals and values subsystem

In all organizations, large or small, there are values—how people think about issues or things. The values enter the organization from the external socio-cultural environment and they are the basis on which decisions are made regarding the philosophy, mission and goals (group and individual). Factors such as the quantity and quality of goods and services to be provided and the specific group of customers to be targeted are all determined within this subsystem.

The technical subsystem

This refers to the knowledge and skills applied to the process of achieving goals, the technology used in the transformation process, the equipment and the facilities. The technical subsystem in each organization is shaped by the tasks it is required to

50

perform. Goals and values determine technological requirements, including knowledge and skills, and technology has a direct impact on goals and objectives.

Structural subsystem

This subsystem is concerned with the process of dividing tasks, allocating them to individuals and groups and establishing relationships between them. The structural subsystem is integrally bound to the technical and the goals and values subsystems. Structure should be based on the purpose (goals) and the relationships in the structure will be a result of the techniques. For example, 'production line' processes use a 'flat' structure that has fewer levels of management, while specialized processes tend to have a taller structure (ie, a longer chain of command). Decision-making centres and authority relationships are also changed with the introduction of new technology.

In the systems flow, changes in these subsystems can set off chain reactions in the psychosocial subsystem, as individuals become dislocated from their usual positions.

The psychosocial subsystem

This subsystem is related to the "human side of the enterprise". It consists of the perceptions, attitudes, behavior and motivation, which are the responses of people in organizations. Group dynamics and interpersonal relationships set the general 'tone' or 'climate' of the organization. Because of the unpredictability of human nature, the management of this subsystem can present a real challenge to managers. Any change in the goals or technical subsystem will naturally affect the structure of the organization, which in turn can lead to changes in attitudes and behavior.

The managerial subsystem

The managerial subsystem is the 'rudder' that guides the organizational 'ship'. It is in this subsystem that the organization's internal system is maintained in a state of equilibrium, while the relationship between the organization as a subsystem in the general organizational supra-system is kept in balance. Managers have responsibility for setting strategic and operational goals, planning for goal attainment, designing the organization structure, making adjustments to the technology and controlling the human relations conflicts.

The Contingency Approach

The contingency approach to management developed out of the findings of systems theorists. The 'contingency' or structural approach put forward the view that, because of the changing nature of the interactions and dynamic interrelationships between the various parts of a system, no 'one best way' of managing an organization could be applied to every situation. The manager should, therefore, select the techniques that are consistent with the needs of a particular situation.

Between the 1940s and late 1960s, several studies carried out in different types of industrial organizations in the United States and Great Britain established the view that the mechanistic principles of management were not universally applicable. The label 'contingency approach' was developed by Lawrence and Lorsch, two researchers from Harvard University, who concluded from their studies that there was no 'one best way' to structure an organization.

They concluded that dynamic and diverse environments require more differential structures than in stable and less-changeable ones. Among other famous studies that drew more or less the same conclusion were those carried out by Burns and Stalker in Scotland and England in the 1950s, who were credited to have influenced the Lawrence and Lorsch study.

The contingency approach does not discriminate against the earlier approaches to management, but rather integrates them into the process by selecting the most appropriate course of action. The manager may make use of the techniques of the classical or behavioral schools in search of an acceptable solution to a problem. In practising the contingency approach, therefore, the emphasis should be on diagnosis or analysis of each situation.

The main conclusions drawn from these and other relevant researchers collectively indicate that there are three basic considerations that should determine the selection of a management approach:

- The organization's goals and objectives
- The available technology
- The environment or situation

Organizational goals and objectives are paramount in the process. It is here suggested that the structure of the organization should follow (or be determined by) the strategy that is developed to meet the goals. When the structure no longer contributes to the achievement of these goals, then the structure should be changed.

The *technology* that is being used is also a critical determinant of the form and structure of the organization. The nature of the work being done and the tasks required to do it, are important considerations when selecting a management structures. Simple production processes can be carried out through a 'flat' structure (ie, with few authority levels, easy communication lines and/or wider spans of control).

In more complex processes, 'tall' structures are required with more reporting levels and often require narrower spans of control. The skills and knowledge of employees are also important factors of technology to be included in determining organizational structure.

The nature of the environment in which the organization operates is also an important factor to be considered in selecting a structure. Relatively stable environments, in which conditions are placid and predictable, favour the more permanent and bureaucratic structural forms of classical theorists. Unstable and turbulent environments on the other hand need more flexibility in their structure in order to facilitate a quick response to changes within and outside the organization.

Summary and Conclusions

Unlike the previous approaches to management, the contingency approach does not advocate a universally correct approach to solving management problems, but maintains that different problems will require different solutions. The contingency approach allows the manager to choose from the available management techniques to solve a problem. This approach is eclectic and requires that the manager be flexible, not locked into any one solution or school of management thought. It allows a concern for the human dimension of the organization as well as the use of operations research techniques. Since this approach requires a manager to view the organization and its problems from a multifaceted point of view, it realistically reflects the complex nature of modern management. It is distinguished by a problem-solving methodology that begins with a situational analysis and ends with the generation, evaluation and recommendation of a potential solution to a management problem.

Critics of the contingency approach stress the complexity of the approach and the fact that it requires a manager of many abilities to use this approach effectively. Many managers will feel insecure, since this approach does not have a set prescription for universal problem-solving, but places the responsibility for solution-generation upon the manager. There are those critics who also maintain that this approach lacks a coherent and consistent theoretical basis and is merely a methodology making use of other approaches. Notwithstanding the credibility of some of these criticisms, it cannot be denied that the contingency approach has the potential to be used creatively, particularly when managing times of great change.

References

Trist, E.A. & Bamforth, K.W (1990) "Some Social and Psychological Consequences of the Longwall Method of Coal-getting", in D.S. Pugh ed., *Organization Theory,* pp. 393-416, (Penguin Business, London).

Kast, Fremont E, & Rosenzweig, James E. (1985) *Organization and Management: A System and Contingency Approach*, 4th ed., pp. 102-121 (McGraw-Hill Book Company, New York).

Robin, Stephen P. (1976) *The Administrative Process: Integrating Theory and Practice*, pp. 271-273 Prentice Hall, Englewood Cliffs, New Jersey).

Lawrence, Paul R. & Lorsch, J.W. (1967) *Organization and Environment* (Harvard Business School, Division of Research, Boston, Mass.).

Woodward, Joan (1965) *Industrial Organization, Theory and Practice* (Oxford University Press, New York).

Burns, Tom & Stalker, G.M. (1961) *The Management of Innovation* (Travistock, Publications, London).

Cole, G.A. (1994) *Management, Theory and Practice*, 4th ed., (D.D. Publication, London).

Toffler, Alvin (1970) *The Third Wave*, (Marrow, New York).

Toffler, Alvin (1960) *Future Shock* (Banton Books, New York).

Drucker, Peter (1995) *Managing in a Time of Great Change* (Penguin Books Ltd., England)

Online Resource

Vector Study.com: Your Gateway to the Management World. Contingency School of Management, www.vectorstudy.com/management_schools/contingency_school.htm

Techniques of Administration and Management

Introduction: From Intuition to a Rational Approach

In the study of the history of the development of management it is observed that, for centuries, men and women carried out their productive activities by trial and error, and made decisions based on 'rule of thumb', intuition and judgment. Theorists from the classical and neoclassical schools described and prescribed and set out guiding principles for moving from nonrational to rational approaches to management. The behavioral theorists took the process further along by pointing out the need to move from a mechanistic to a humanistic approach. However, these theorists did not provide any detail about how to apply the principles to the practice, except in a general and often contradictory way.

In this section, the skills necessary for performing management tasks as well as some detailed methods for applying those skills to each function (element) of management will be discussed.

In general, the skills required for performing management tasks are

- Conceptual
- Technical
- Human relations
- Critical thinking

The guidelines for acquiring these skills are included in the theoretical framework of this text.

Conceptual Skills

Knowledge of the substantive or peculiar problems of the organization is essential for every manager in the performance of his or her tasks.

Every organization has specific problems (eg, problems in the health sector are different from those in the education and housing sectors). Although some of these problems overlap, each sector manager is expected to be proficient in the substantive aspects of the job. A manager must be knowledgeable about the organization's policies and procedures, the nature of the services offered and the range of problems associated with the management of the organization. It is also a requirement that all managers are familiar with the legal framework within which the organization operates.

Conceptual skills are developed through

- the continuous study of problems of organization in the same field;
- subscription to professional journals, periodicals and the like; and
- attendance at local, regional and international conferences, and the like, where substantive issues are discussed.

Technical Skills

All managers are required to possess technical skills of a general nature, which are applicable to the management of large-scale organizations. The earliest management theorists provided a systematic formulation of these general techniques. They provided the basis for understanding how to order and direct the structure and processes that will contribute to the achievement of goals and objectives. These theorists (who were referred to as classical theorists) provided the foundation for establishing the link between the theories and techniques of management.

Human-Relations Skills

All managers must be knowledgeable about human behavior, and possess human-relations skills that equip them to lead employees to direct their efforts and to motivate them to contribute to the achievement of the organizational goals. They must possess the ability to communicate effectively with members of their staff as well as others within the organization. These skills are also required when interacting with stakeholders outside the organization—clients, suppliers, benefactors and those whose inputs contribute to the organization's efficiency and effectiveness. There is a large body of work on human relations and behavioral theories that contributes to an understanding and development of these skills. Some of these works are included in the theoretical framework of this text.

Critical-Thinking Skills

Critical thinking is an essential part of the management process because it integrates and encompasses the other skills—conceptual, technical and human-relations skills. Critical thinking involves such qualitative concepts as insight, intuition and empathy. The methodology for applying critical thinking is reflective, analytical and oriented to problem-solving in an 'open' system rather than a 'closed' system approach to management, in which solutions to organizational problems are prescribed as 'givens'.

This section of the text provides a framework for the development of the knowledge and skills required to carry out the activities of management. While theories set our general principles of management in a scientific way, techniques provide the tools that the manager uses to practice the 'art' of management.

In discussing the techniques that are applicable to the main functions or processes of management, various theoretical perspectives, which were examined in the previous section, will be re-examined. The techniques to be discussed are decision-making, planning, organizing, directing (commanding) and controlling (evaluating).

Reference

Lupton, Tom (1983), *Management and the Social Sciences*, (Penguin Books Ltd., London).

Online Resources

Human Resource Management blog, http://management-rec.blogspot.com/

Union Divided: Business Tips and Tricks blog, http://www.uniondivided.com/business-management/management

Decision-Making

Introduction: Decision-Making Throughout the Organization

Decision-making, which has been defined as "making a choice between alternatives", is widely accepted as an activity in which everyone is involved. The importance of effective decision-making was first discussed by the classical theorist Frederick Taylor. At the turn of the 20th century, Taylor stated that managerial decisions were based on 'rule of thumb' evaluations or intuition. He, therefore, set out to develop a scientific approach to management that would, inter alia, achieve rationality in all aspects of the decision-making process. Over the decades, the development of all aspects of the decision-making technique has moved along a continuum from simple 'nonrational' to complex 'rational' approaches.

Types of Decisions

The types of decisions made by individuals and groups in organizations will vary according to the decision-maker's position within the structure of the organization.

Some distinctions have been made between the types of decisions made in any organization. One of the theoretical distinctions is between decisions concerning 'ends' and decisions concerning 'means'. Decisions about 'ends' are those that are reached from what is referred to as 'value' premises. When making these decisions, the decision-makers use judgment to determine what, for example, should be the organization's goals, philosophy or mission. They seek to establish what ought to be. Since value premises vary from one person to another, decisional outputs based on these premises also vary and are often the cause of conflict in the decision-making process. Some important organizational decisions that are based on value premises include

- organizational objectives,
- criteria on which standards of efficiency are judged, and
- standards of fair play.

59

Decisions about 'means' are based on 'factual' premises. The decisions are based on concrete issues and require more detailed consideration and focus on what 'is'. Information used in formulating such decisions is found in organizational records, existing rules and regulations and other forms of hard data. The decision-makers must, therefore, be more diligent in their search for decisional inputs and must give thought to such questions as

- what resources are available to implement the decision,

- how much will implementation cost,

- who will implement the decision, and

- when and where will the process take place

Sometimes there is no clear line of demarcation between 'value' premises and 'factual' premises; and sometimes what appears to be 'factual' could be 'value-laden', because of the influence that an individual's socialization might have on the decision-making process.

Categories of Decision

Decisions may also be categorized on the basis of the role that relationships play within and between the decision-makers. These categories include strategic decisions, administrative decisions and operating decisions.

Strategic decisions are those that pertain to the relationship between the organization and its external environment. These decisions are usually made by senior-level officials in interaction with national, regional or international organizations. Decisions that include the organization's relationship with others in the same task environment also are made at the strategic level.

Administrative decisions, also referred to as 'organizational decisions', are concerned with the conversion of a strategic decision into structures and processes for implementation. They include such decisions as

- establishing programmes,

- structuring authority relationships, and

- determining work flow

These decisions are usually made by second-level managers (also referred to as administrators) in the organization.

Operating decisions also called 'line' decisions are, as the term implies, taken at the point of operation. These are routine decisions concerned with such issues as the maintenance of output, productivity, pricing and inventory. Many operational decisions have to be made on the spur of the moment and in response to environmental changes.

Programmed and Non-Programmed Decisions

It is possible to further distinguish between two polar types of decisions—'programmed' and 'non-programmed'. Herbert Simon (1976), in discussing how executives make decisions, made the point that it would be more accurate to consider these two categories as merely two extremes on a continuum, the distinction between them often being one of degree.

Decisions are programmed to the extent that

- they are repetitive and routine, and

- a definite procedure has been worked out for handling them so that they do not have to be treated as a new problem each time they occur.

All organizations have programmed decisions that permit them to respond promptly to routine situations. Certain rules and regulations and standard operating procedures are programmed decisions. Organizations tend to improve their performance by increasing the areas of activity that are covered by programmed decisions.

Decisions are non-programmed to the extent that they are new, unstructured and consequential. That is to say, there is no cut-and-dried method for handling the problem because it has not arisen before, or it is so important that it deserves a custom-tailored treatment. What is being sought on the occasion of a non-programmed decision is a decisional response in which the system has no specific procedure for dealing with a situation like the one on hand, but must rely on whatever general capacity exists for intelligent, adaptive problem-oriented action.

Steps in the Decision-Making Process

Administrative decisions are made within the context of the goals and objectives of the organization and are intended to solve a management problem. A problem may be defined as a situation that is not in congruence with a desired state within the context of the organization's philosophy and mission. A problem may also be identified as an incident that occurred in the past (as a result of a set of circumstances) and that are likely to recur under similar conditions. A problem may also be a projected event, based on trends that have been identified as a result of scientific research.

To achieve rationality in the process of decision-making, the following linear steps are recommended:

Step 1: Define the Problem
Correctly identifying and defining the problem is the first step in the decision-making process. Failure to make a right decision is often the result of mistaking a symptom for the problem.

Defining the problem should start with the question about the desired state, and this activity should not be limited to the perception, values or frame of reference of the manager. Neither should this process be completely influenced by special interests within the organization.

Step 2: Collect Relevant Information About the Problem
After the problem has been identified, care should be taken to gather detailed information about the problem, making use of well-known information-gathering techniques—both formal and informal. The approach to gathering information will depend, to a large extent, on the type of problem and the time available to find a solution.

Step 3: Classify and Analyse the Data

In this process, distinction must be made between information based on value premises and those based on facts. Tools that are useful in classification of data include graphs and charts. Comparing new information with what already exists in files, records and personal memory will assist in determining the relevance of the data.

Analysis must point out areas of incoherence and inconsistencies in the information, bearing in mind, for example, that the cultural environment can have a significant effect on the quality of the information collected.

Step 4: Prepare a List of Alternative Solutions

The list of alternative solutions should include past approaches to the same or similar problems within the organization. Information should also be collected on the ways in which other groups and organizations have dealt with similar problems. This process will facilitate the selection of the best possible alternative.

Step 5: Evaluate the Consequences of Each Alternative

In this step a 'cost and benefit analysis' of each selected alternative should be carried out to ensure that the decision comes as close as possible to rationality. Some of the factors to be considered when evaluating alternatives are as follows:

- The element of risk involved in each alternative and the potential for positive or negative outcomes in human, economic, social or other costs or benefits.

- The extent to which implementation of each alternative will solve the problem, with minimum disruption of the problem area as well as other parts of the organization.

- The alternative that will make best use of available resources—people, equipment and other capital.

In evaluating alternatives, the role of personal intuition should not be underestimated. This element in the decision-making process has been given theoretical credibility in the 'extra-national' approach to decision-making. This is particularly important in environments where there is a tendency for respondents to 'colour' information or withhold important facts for reasons of privacy, as part of a cultural norm.

Step 6: Select a Solution

The selection of a solution is the ultimate purpose of the decision-making process. Although this step is the result of a long process, the selection of a solution is not an end in itself. In the real world, the solution selected will not necessarily be an optimum one, but will be 'bounded' by constraints identified in the theory of decision-making. As a result, other decisions will have to be made to solve other problems that are unintended consequences of the decision chosen.

Step 7: Implement the Decision

Implementation of the decision is as important to the management process as the decision-making process itself. At this stage, relevant members of the organization should become part of the process to ensure that the decision produces the anticipated outcome. All the elements of management—planning, organizing, directing and controlling—must constantly be included in the implementation of an administrative decision.

Step 8: Measuring the Results

The only way of ensuring that a decision that is being implemented is in tandem with the stated objectives is to conduct continuous measurement of the results. Unexpected events can change the expected outcome of the implementation of a decision. Measuring results provides an opportunity to re-examine any of the steps taken so that adjustments can be made to any part of the process at any time.

This phasal structure of the decision-making process is only a template and does not suggest that the steps must be followed rigidly. It merely points to the dependence of one stage of the process on the previous one. In reality, the manager/decision-maker may have to re-examine a previous step as new information emerges, thereby requiring more analysis and evaluation. Thus, feedback at different phases in the process will assist in the clarification of issues and help to close the boundary between rational and irrational decisions.

In general, these steps in rational decision-making represent an ideal situation. It is clear, however, that the process must, of necessity, be nonlinear, in view of the high level of risk and uncertainty that would be integral to each step. Decision-making theorists have argued about the capacity of decision-makers to achieve any degree of rationality, in view of the limitations of the several human and material factors involved in the process.

Decision-Making Techniques

Several techniques have been developed to assist the decision-maker to more precisely predict the future. Among these techniques or tools are the following:

Operations Research (OR) or Management Science. This highly quantitative technique, which is influenced by general systems theory, involves the use of scientific models to simulate real situations. Some OR techniques include Network Analysis, Risk Analysis and Statistical Decision Theory. Among the benefits that derive from these techniques is their capability to produce information and evaluations that can improve the quality of solutions to problems within the organization.

Decision Tree. Another decision-making tool that has grown in significance is the 'decision tree'. The decision tree is a conceptual map on which the possible decisions and outcomes in a given situation are displayed. The decision tree depicts each alternative strategy like a branch on a tree and assigns a value to the probability of some event occurring in the future. By weighting the value of each probable outcome, a comparison can be made between possible choices and a decision chosen from the list of possible alternatives.

Managers who are required to make a number of sequential decisions under conditions where earlier decisions will affect later ones would find this decision-making tool very effective. In applying techniques, managers can be ably assisted by skilled mathematicians, statisticians and information technology (IT) specialists.

Breakdown Analysis. This technique is usually employed in productive enterprises that are in search of a breakeven point between costs and revenues. The limitation of this technique is that it assumes an element of predictability and stability in the decision-making environment and follows closely the rational comprehensive model of decision-making.

Brainstorming. This is another non-quantifiable technique, which was designed to allow groups in an organization to creatively think through a problem and arrive at an optimum decision. Originally, this technique was developed as a means of solving advertising problems, but has been extended to include the different types of decision-making situations.

Brainstorming has been criticized for its limited capacity to reach decisions on complex issues within a short time. However, it has been found to be useful in arriving at decisions on some simple organizational problems, especially in situations where there is a high level of cohesiveness among participants in the decision-making process.

Summary and Conclusions

Recognition of the role of decision-making in the management process is a priority concern of administrative theory. Although all members of the organization make decisions, there are differences in the categories of decisions made at different levels of the organization. However, it is important that, at whatever level the decision-maker is operating, the objective should be to achieve the highest net benefit in the interest of the objectives of the organization and to ensure that there is 'unity of direction'. The steps that are identified in the decision-making process are intended to help the decision-maker to improve the quality of the decision. Over time, some new techniques have been developed with the objective of improving organizational decision-making. In spite of the increase in technology and its widespread use in data gathering and the selection of alternatives, people in organizations play a very important role in the decision-making process and therefore need to have some knowledge of what is required to make rational decisions.

References

Cole, G.A. (1990) *Management: Theory and Practice,* 3rd ed., pp. 108–113 (ELBA – DP Publications, London).

Simon, Herbert A. (1960) *The New Science of Management Decision* (Harper & Brothers Publications, New York).

Robins, Stephen P. & Coulter, Mary (1966) *Management,* 6th ed., chap. 6 (Prentice Hall, New York).

Hampton, David R. (1981) *Contemporary Management,* 2nd ed., chap. 7 (McGraw Hill, New York).

National Institute of Business Management (1993) *The Step-by-Step Approach for Success,* pp. 23-44 (Berkley Books, New York).

Luthans, Fred (1977) *The Decision Process Organizational Behaviour,* International Student Edition, chap. 8 (McGraw Hill, New York).

Online Resources

Simple Processes for Problem-Solving and Decision-Making, http://www.businessballs.com/problemsolving.htm

Decision-making Techniques: How to Make Better Decisions. Mind Tools: Essential Skills for an Excellent Career, http://www.mindtools.com/pages/main/newMN_TED.htm

Planning

Introduction: The Definitions

There are several definitions of planning. One of the simplest is that planning is a process in which a series of decisions are taken in advance about what is to be done and how it is to be done. Henri Fayol, the theorist who developed the five elements of management, used the term 'prevoyance', which means forecasting or assessing where the present course of action will lead. Planning is also defined as an activity that involves decisions about 'ends' (where we want to go), and 'means' (how to get there)—the principles which will guide the process (policies) and the standards for evaluating the results (control). From these definitions, it will be observed that planning and decision-making are closely associated.

Reasons for Planning

There is a saying that "if you fail to plan, then you plan to fail". While planning does not automatically guarantee success in accomplishing organizational goals, the absence of a plan is a sure way of limiting a manager's success. There are at least five critical reasons why managers should plan.

1. Planning affects performance

Empirical studies have shown that those enterprises, whether public or private, that engage in planning show superior performance over those that do not. Similarly, individuals who engage in planning have a better chance of improving their performance at any task.

2. Planning focuses attention on objectives

Setting objectives is an important part of the planning process. When it has been decided where the organization wishes to go, in other words, when decisions are made about ends, the planning process must include decisions about how to achieve those ends. Those are the means decisions and planning helps in unifying and directing all the actions of the participants in the organization who are working towards the same ends. Thus, planning helps the organization to achieve unity of direction.

3. Planning helps to reduce risks

Every management situation is prone to risks, because the environment is constantly subjected to change. It is important in planning to collect information in order to forecast the future. In the process, plans can include decisions that make provision for the possibility of change. While change is certain, the manager can reduce risks by making plans for the foreseeable future. With the improvements in technology, the techniques for planning for the future have been enhanced, and the modern manager can make contingency plans as events occur and circumstances change.

4. Planning improves efficiency

Managers at any level in the organization can improve efficiency; that is, they can minimize the cost of operations through planning. This is done by integrating the different activities that make up the work plan. As a result, more can be achieved with less effort. The more complex the organization, the more importance planning assumes as a means of maximizing the use of resources, cutting cost and avoiding the duplication of effort. The exchange of information on the daily plan within and between departments or units can contribute significantly to improving the efficiency of both managers and employees.

5. Planning facilitates control

At the planning stage, standards of performance are set so that there can be continual analysis and measurement of actual outputs against the results that were anticipated and desired. Planning provides the basis of the development of warning signals whenever the plan is going off track. Planning determines the information needed to set the standards (what is to be achieved) and the time frame within which the measurement should take place. In addition, the planning process determines the scope of the manager's responsibility and accountability and the standards by which effectiveness is evaluated.

Fundamentals of Good Planning

There are certain general characteristics that should be incorporated in an effective plan of action. These are as follows:

Unity: All formal organizations have different component parts, each having its own plans of action. However, the actions taken in each part must be directed towards the objective of the super-ordinate plan. Unity of direction is a fundamental principle of management of large organizations.

Continuity: There must be in each plan provision for continuity, to ensure that each activity is moving towards its final goal. Inconsistencies in plan implementation are to be avoided as much as possible if a plan is to be effective in making optimum use of all the organization's resources.

Flexibility: A good action plan must be flexible. It must include capability to adapt to inevitable changes, which often occur in both the organization's internal and external environments.

Precision: Precision in planning sets the standards against which to measure outcomes, to evaluate performance and to take corrective action where necessary.

Categories of Planning

There are several different categories in which plans may be classified. For example:

- A plan may be categorized by its time frame (ie, long term, intermediate or short term).

- A long-term plan may have a time frame of three to five years. However, some plans have longer time frames, such as development plans, which may be set for 10 to 20 years.

- Short-term plans are often set for a period of one year or less, and a number of short-term plans may be developed in succession to become intermediate range to long term. If, for example, a short-term plan has not been fully executed at the end of a period, or if the need for continuation arises, that plan can be rolled over until it is fully implemented.

- The 'use dimension' of a plan is another category. For example, a plan may be developed for a single use, such as a budget for a project or a 'standing plan' that provides a framework for activities that are performed over and over again. Policies, rules and regulations that are established as programmed decisions are standing plans.

There are two general categories of planning that focus on the 'scope' and 'breadth' dimension of the plan. They are as follows:

Strategic Planning

These are concerned with the setting of long-term goals of the organization and are developed to address general strategic problems such as

- where is the organization at present,

- where should the organization be at a given future time,

- what specific goals should be achieved, and

- by what means should they be met.

Strategic plans are generally about 'ends', and are usually conceived within the framework of some development goals. Strategic plans, which incorporate strategic decision-making, establish the relationship between the organization and its external environment. This category of planning usually takes place at the senior level of the organization. However, depending on such factors as the size of the organization, the nature of the services being offered and the levels of decentralization, strategic planning may be done by middle managers and includes inputs from lower-level staff. At whatever level the strategic planning takes place, care must be taken to ensure that it fits in with the overall developmental goals of the organization. This ensures that there is unity of direction in planning.

Operational Planning

Operational planning (sometimes referred to as 'tactical planning') places emphasis on how the strategic plan is to be accomplished. In the process of operational planning, the general ideas formulated in the strategic plan are translated into more specific terms that entail making detailed short-term decisions. The three main elements of the operational plan are as follows:

1. Strategies that describe how each goal will be achieved. At this stage, the steps in the decision-making process will be followed to ensure that the most efficient and effective strategy is selected from several alternative strategies that are available.

2. Objectives that are statements of the specific results to be achieved, when they will be started and completed, and by whom.

3. Targets that are set to measure the performance of staff as well as to determine whether the objectives of the program are being met. Targets to be met must be expressed in specific quantitative terms, where possible. Where numerical values are not available, the qualitative terms of measurement of the targets should be clearly stated.

Corporate Planning

The term 'corporate planning' is used to describe a planning technique that is designed to ensure that the overall purpose, goals, strategies and objectives of the organization are focused in the same direction. It is also a style of management that is used to involve all the organizational units in the planning process to ensure that all the major functions of the organization are managed in the interest of the general good.

Steps in the Planning Process

The planning process consists of a number of practical steps that are set out as guidelines (rather than rules) that a manager may follow in order to achieve the overall planning objective.

Step 1: Identify the Current Mission, Strategies and Objectives of the Organization

The organization's mission statement, which is derived from the philosophy on which the organization is established, is a general statement of the type of organization, its purpose and its values. The philosophy represents the 'ideal' on which the organization is founded. A mission statement defines the purpose of the organization—the reason for its existence. The mission statement should be clear, relatively brief and to the point and should present the members of the organization and general public with a word picture of its objectives and the strategies that will be employed for their achievement.

In preparing the mission statement, there should be consultation with members of the organization to ensure that the essential aspects of the organization's values are incorporated in the statement.

Step 2: Analyse the External Environment

In the systems approach to management, consideration is given to the high level of interdependence between the organization and its external environment. Some critical factors that should be included in this environmental analysis are as follows:

Culture. The cultural norms and values, which are the very fabric of the external environment, include the system of beliefs that influence the patterns of interpersonal relationships, patterns of authority and leadership. The culture also includes the elements of daily living (eg, religion, language, food as well as the nature of social institutions).

Demography. General information about the population or the target group for which the plan has been made should be collected and analysed, including facts on the human population, number, age and gender distribution. (In some organizations information about race and ethnicity, birth and death rates, morbidity, etc. like may also be relevant.)

Patterns of migration and immigration are demographic factors as well as the concentration of the population between urban and rural areas. These are also important (again, depending on the mission).

Politics. Information on certain political characteristics of the environment is very important for analysis. The nature of the general political climate, political organizations and the distribution of political power among the general population should be included in the knowledge base for effective planning.

The legal and constitutional framework is also an important political consideration.

Economics. The economic characteristics of the environments to be analysed include the types of structures and activities of economic organizations (eg, banks, insurance companies, etc.). Knowledge of the pattern of economic ownership as between public and private sectors, the levels of investment in capital resources and patterns of consumption are also important.

Information about the level of employment, net income and amount of disposable income in families is also relevant.

Labour Market. The labour supply in the external environment is another important factor to be analysed, so as to ascertain the organization's ability to compete for human resources with rivals in the same task environment.

Step 3: Analyse the Internal Environment

In-depth analyses of the organization's internal environment should then be carried out. Important factors to be considered include the following:

Management capabilities. This analysis should focus on the ability of the management team to perform the management functions of planning, organizing, leading and controlling.

Resource sufficiency. The actual analysis should provide information about adequacy of the organization's human and material resources. With respect to human resources, the staff complement, the adequacy of their training, the levels of their motivation and commitment to the mission and goals of the organization should be evaluated.

With respect to material resources, there should be concern about the availability, quantity and appropriateness of the technology and working space for effective operation. The organization's access to financial resources is also an important consideration in this analysis.

Organization Culture. The culture of the internal organization is an important factor to be analysed. The values, beliefs, attitudes, patterns of behavior (described as "the way we do things") and their impact on the process of getting things done should be carefully analysed. In this respect, the influence of the informal organization is an environmental factor to be carefully considered.

Step 4: Conduct a Strength, Weakness, Opportunity, Threat (SWOT) Analysis

A SWOT analysis is a process to determine the organization's internal strengths and weaknesses and its external opportunities and threats.

Internal strengths include those activities that the organization does well—that show high levels of achievement of the organization's goals. Weaknesses, on the other hand, relate to those activities that the organization does not do well and that compare unfavourably with their competitors.

In terms of human resources, a strength would be the ability to attract and retain a skilled workforce, while a weakness would be high staff turnover.

In terms of material resources, a strength would be the ability to attract investment capital and practice prudent financial management. A weakness would be the opposite of these elements.

An internal cultural strength is one in which employees are positively committed and work cooperatively to achieve the goals of the organization, while a weakness would be one in which their management-worker relationship is personified by confrontation.

The external environmental opportunities are those in which the organization can improve on its own strengths by merging or cooperating with other organizations that have specialized capabilities. Threats (also referred to as challenges) are those elements in the external environment that might require the organization to re-evaluate its mission and objectives. This is the point in the process at which a manager assesses whether the original plan is realistic or whether modifications should be made.

Step 5: Establish Goals

After completing a comprehensive analysis of those factors in the internal and external environments that would have an impact on the implementation process, the next step is to set goals. The goals are the ends that the plans are designed to achieve. Goals are sometimes referred to as 'aims'.

There are different levels of goal-setting; each level is determined by the position of the plan in the planning hierarchy. The importance of goal-setting at each level is to ensure that there is unity of direction (ie, goals at the lower levels of the organization are in congruence with the goals at the higher levels).

Step 6: Formulate Strategies to Achieve Goals

Strategies are developed at the operational level, to determine the route to be taken to reach the goals. This step in the process is aimed at finding the strategy that will lead to achievement of planned goals with the lowest net cost in time, material and human resources. This phase of planning should always be carried out with input from other members of the organization. Reference should also be made to the programmed decisions that already exist in the organization, through comprehensive search of files and other stored documentation.

- To what extent is it possible for individual and organizational goals to coincide.
- What form of reward should be given for a job well done.
- What effect does MBO have on different cultural and ethnic groups
- How will managers and subordinates react to the self-controlling element of MBO

Skills Required to Perform Planning Function

In order to carry out the planning process, a manager should be able to

- establish a philosophy of management for the organization and write a mission statement;
- forecast future events that are likely to affect the management process;
- analyse the external environment and assess the effects of general environmental characteristics on the organizational task environment;
- analyse the internal organizational environment to determine its strengths and weaknesses;
- establish policies to guide the process of decision-making;
- set long-term and short-term programme goals that define, in general terms, what are the anticipated outcomes for a programme at the end of a specific period;
- define the programmes necessary to achieve the mission;
- establish objectives for the programmes, setting out what is to be done, how and by whom;
- devise schedules of activities to meet the objectives;
- develop budgets, and provide resources to support the programme; and
- establish methods, procedures and a system to ensure uniformity and clarity and provide for evaluation and control.

Summary and Conclusions

Planning is made up of a complex set of activities that involve managers at different levels of the organization. The structure of the organization will determine the category of planning for which a manager is responsible. Depending on the size of the organization, a manager may have responsibility for more than one category. Regardless of the planning focus. However, all plans ought to be part of a unified system and should support the principle of 'unity of direction'. There are several tools and techniques available to the modern manager. One human relations approach is management by objectives.

References:

Cole, G.A. (2003) *Management: Theory and Practice* op. cit., pp. 114-123 (Cengage Learning Business Press, London).

Robbins, Stephen R. & Coulter, Mary (2004) "Foundation of Planning", in *Management*, op. cit., chap. 7, pp. 211-233 (Prentice Hall, London).

Robbins, Stephen R. & Coulter, Mary (2004) "Planning Tools & Techniques", in *Management*, op cit., chap. 9, pp. 267-296 (Prentice Hall, London).

Humble, John (1975) "Avoiding the Pitfalls of MPO – An Introduction to MBO", in *Management by Objectives*, pp. 1-8 (Essex Gower Press, London).

Drucker, Peter (1955) *The Practice of Management* (Heineman, London).

Tosi, Henri L. & Carroll, Stephen (1970) "Management by Objectives", in *Personnel Administration*, vol. 33, pp. 44-48 (McMillian, New York).

Online Resource

Management Study Guide. Principles of Management http://www.managementstudyguide.com/management_principles.htm

Organizing

Introduction

Organizing is the process of dividing tasks, responsibilities and decisions among people and groups, establishing appropriate relationships among people and ensuring that the activities of each person fit together to achieve the objectives that modern management theorists have defined as well as prescribed for the process of organizing. A fundamental principle in the organizing function is that "structure should follow strategy", that is to say that the organization structure should be compatible with the purpose of the plan. Organizing involves three set of decisions:

- Decisions about the division of work
- Decisions about the allocation of authority and responsibility
- Decisions about the coordination of tasks

Theoretical Approaches to Organizing

In the development of management theory, some general principles were set out for organizing or 'structuring' an organization for efficiency. The theorists in this school applied technical principles such as scientific management (Taylor, et al.), bureaucratic or 'ideal' types of organizations (Max Weber) or general principles of administration (Henri Fayol). These approaches are based on the concept of "management by control", in which managers at the senior level of the organization are solely responsible for establishing structures.

With the development of the human relations school, some consideration was given to the needs of people in the organizing process. Allowances were made for more participation in decision-making and planning, upward as well as downward communication, self-appraisal and encouraging informal organizations (or group influence). These changes in approach had some effect on the organization structure, as the system became more open to input from employees.

The development of an open systems approach to management further influenced the organizing process, although the extent to which this approach has gained wide acceptance will vary from one organization to another.

The Contingency Approach

The modern approach to organizing is the contingency approach, which takes the environment, the goals and objectives and the availability of appropriate technology into consideration. In this approach the nature of the environment is considered to be important in structuring an organization. For example, environments that are relatively stable and in which conditions are predictable favour more permanent or bureaucratic organization structures. Unstable turbulent environments in which conditions are constantly changing and are subject to material disasters need more flexibility in their form.

In the contingency approach, the best organization structure is one that fits the goals, strategies and objectives to be met, and it follows that any change in the organization strategy should be followed by a change in its structure.

In the contingency approach to organizing, the technology is also a critical factor in determining the form or structure of the organization. Simple production processes can be performed through flat structures, with fewer levels of authority, while complex processes require tall structures and more reporting levels, more division of labour and, under some conditions, narrower spans of control.

Despite the different perspectives on organizing, it is a given that all organizations, large or small, require a structure within which all activities are rationally performed. The techniques or approaches applied in organizing will vary from one situation to another—a structure may evolve through "habit and practice" or may be formally designed. Organization structures are not cast in stone but may, over time, be subject to change as changing conditions demand. Thus, 're-organizing' is also a technique in the organizing process.

Types of Organization Structure

There are several different types of organization structure, each of which may be considered more appropriate to meet the needs of a contingency approach. Each type of structure has both positive and negative aspects. Consequently, the role of management is to ensure that the negative aspects are kept to the minimum and managed in the best interest of the total organization.

The Functional Organization

This is a structure in which all the activities to be performed are divided according to their functions (ie, each unit or department is responsible for all similar functions or activities that are required to achieve the organization's goals and objectives).

Most large organizations that perform functions of central administration are structured as functional organizations.

Structure of the Functional Organization

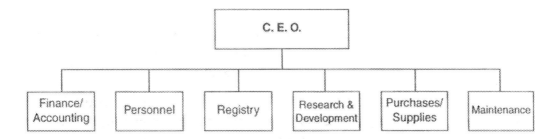

Advantages of the functional organization

Each individual in the functional organization has only to be concerned with one kind of work (eg, the accountant can focus on accounting without having to spend much time on non-accounting functions).

This structure allows each person to become more competent by performing each task repeatedly. He or she also has the support of others in the same kind of work who are able to offer specialized assistance in the solution of problems (eg, junior members of staff in the personnel department can ask for the help of senior staff members in matters of appointments, salaries, leave and so on). Functional organizations also provide better opportunities for career development and promotion.

When environmental conditions are stable, the demand for goods and services tends to remain constant. The functional structure allows for the assignment of one individual to meet these demands, thus maximizing the use of their efforts. For example, in a purchasing department the officer who processes goods from a special supplier will know almost every peculiarity of that company and is, therefore, better able to carry out that function.

Disadvantages of the functional organization

Some disadvantages will result from the functional organizational structure. There is a tendency for staff members in a functional unit to be more concerned with their own special jobs and they may fail to cooperate with others. For example, the maintenance department might delay the repairs in another department without any consideration for the needs of that department. Similarly, staff in the personnel department may be concerned about applying personnel rules and regulations to an appointment but fail to send relevant information to the accounts department so that salaries and other emoluments can be paid on time.

Sometimes the objectives of one department are not in tandem with the objectives of another and this creates a conflict of interest. The accountant is interested in staying within the budget and another department head is concerned with the acquisition of the most modern technology. It is very difficult to get people to work together when their objectives are at variance with one another.

In a turbulent environment, the functional organization might prove to be disadvantageous because cooperation in these circumstances is absolutely necessary, especially when adjustments have to be made very quickly.

The Product or Project Organization

This is an organization structure in which the work is divided based on the product. That means that each division of the total organization has responsibility for an entire product or output. In this structure, teams or groups are required to work together to achieve segments of the whole programme. The person in charge—the programme/product manager—of this decentralized organization has responsibility for the functions required to achieve its specific objectives. An example of this structure would be a job classification unit of a personnel department, which is given the task of collecting data for job analysis and reclassification of staff. A programme director (PD) would be the person in charge of the unit and would have specially assigned duties. Another example would be a large construction company that separates the building of houses into low-income and prestige homes.

Advantages of the product/project organization

The advantages of this structure are as follows:

- More cooperation among workers. Because staff can identify with an output/product they tend to be more motivated to successfully complete the tasks.

- There is more opportunity for innovation and creativity and there is more communication as the chain of command tends to be shorter.

- It is much easier to make adjustments to changes, as the regulations tend to be less structured. This structure is, therefore, more suitable for less-stable environments.

- The performance indicators can be more easily defined and responsibility and accountability rest with the programme manager.

Disadvantages of the product/project organization

There are some disadvantages in this organization structure, which can easily be seen as the advantages in a functional organization.

- There is often a lack of opportunity for the development of specialized skills and competence. Staff in a product or programme organization may have to work at different tasks in order to get the job done within a given time frame. This, of course, will depend on the overall size of the company and the opportunities for continuous employment.

- The job tenure is less secure and employees may not concentrate on the tasks as diligently as they would in the functional organization. In some public development projects in underdeveloped states, there is a tendency for staff members to delay the completion of a project because of uncertainty about their future employment. This can result in time and cost overruns. Again, this might not be the case where there is employment of skilled workers, as they will always be able to find jobs.

The Geographical or Territorial Organization

This is a decentralized structure, as in a product or project organization. However, the division is done on a regional basis and is usually adopted in order to overcome some of the administrative problems of over-centralization. In such cases, centres of decision making and control over human and material resources are removed from the capital city to regional centres. Each regional manager is responsible for all the functions that fall within his or her area.

Advantages of the geographical or territorial organization

The geographical organization allows the group to make decisions, set goals and plan to meet the specific needs of a region. This structure allows for speedy decisions to be made at the location of a problem rather than going through the long chain of command from periphery to centre. It also gives recognition to the importance of environmental considerations.

Disadvantages of the geographical or territorial organization

A disadvantage of the regional organization structure is the possibility of misinterpretation of the overall goals by those in the periphery. There is also room for a deliberate changing of the focus of plans to fit the specialized interests of the regional manager.

We will now look at a fourth structure, one which has become increasingly popular with the increased complexity and size of organizations.

The Matrix Organization

The matrix organization is one that combines the features of functional, product, geographical or any other organizational structure. It is also referred to as a composite structure and it is an attempt to gain the advantages of more than one organization.

Structure of the Matrix Organization

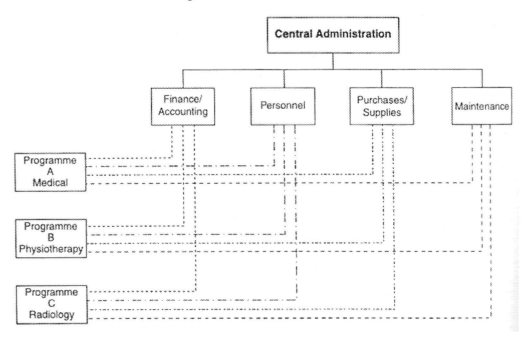

Advantages of the matrix organization

As with other forms, the matrix structure has advantages and disadvantages. A matrix organization draws on the strengths of the functional organization, which encourages the development of specialists who are competent in their job. It also draws on the strength of the product organization, which encourages coordination, creativity and initiative, and focuses on results.

The matrix structure has the advantage in large organizations of allowing groups in the product or programme organization to focus on their substantive (main) functions, while leaving the supportive functions to the staff in the functional structure. This also allows for the benefit of the development of competence through different routes.

- In the functional organization, there are stable operations based on programmed decisions; this leads to the development of staff competence.

- In the product/programme organization, competence is developed through communication—the exchange of ideas among specialists. The groups in this structure have direct contact with the client and concentrate on outputs. They have the opportunity to initiate changes in techniques by being closer to the problem areas, and so are able to respond to crises quickly. They often have to make non-programmed decisions.

Disadvantages of the matrix organization

One of the major disadvantages of the matrix structure is the difficulty that often arises in clarifying authority/responsibility relationships. The head of the functional division has authority over the staff in his or her department to decide on their work schedules and assignments. The head of the programme division has responsibility for the output of his or her unit but does not have the equivalent authority to assign functional tasks to employees in the functional departments. This can create problems and conflicts, especially when the heads of both organizations are unable to work out a satisfactory solution. The matrix structure is one in which authority is not equal to responsibility, as Fayol recommended.

Coordination

When the process of structuring an organization has been completed and the functions have been assigned to specialized areas, another important task is to decide how to make the parts work together. This aspect of the organizing function involves decisions about the coordination of tasks.

A first consideration in coordinating is to decide what activities are to be coordinated and how much coordination is necessary. One of the major weaknesses identified in large-scale organizations is the problem of under-coordination. This occurs when there are inadequate linkages between persons and groups whose jobs are interdependent.

According to Henri Fayol, "to coordinate is to harmonize all the activities of a concern so as to facilitate its proper working and its success".

Mary Parker Follet, a neoclassical theorist stated the following:

> It seems to me that the first test of business administration, of industrial organization, should be whether you have a business with all its parts so coordinated, so moving together in their closely knit and adjusting activities, so inter-locking, inter-relating that they make a working unit.

Techniques of Coordination

In classical theories, organizing principles incorporate the concept of coordination. In the chain of command or scalar chain (Fayol) or the hierarchical structure (Weber) it is prescribed that there should be an unbroken set of reporting relationships from top to bottom of the organization. While some of these principles are still applicable, some have to be modified and subjected to a contingency approach, in order to bring practices in line with changes in the environment as well as the application of new technology. Coordination within and between units may be either vertical (ie, top-down or vice versa) or lateral or horizontal, (ie, among groups or individuals on the same level).

Vertical coordination is maintained through the hierarchical structure or 'chain of command'. According to German sociologist Max Weber (1864–1920), "each person in a position of authority is responsible to the person above for his decisions and actions, and the decisions and actions of those below them". In this scalar chain, each official is responsible and accountable to some superior, thus ensuring vertical coordination. The organization chart provides a visual illustration of the chain of command.

In large, complex organizations, vertical coordination may be maintained by written reports and regularly scheduled meetings between senior line managers (CEOs) and heads of departments to whom authority has been delegated. At these meetings, issues and problems are reported and discussed and decisions are made regarding solutions. Schedules are set for feedback on the outcome of implementation of the decisions.

This coordinating technique can also be applied at the departmental level in meetings between heads of departments and senior supervisors or 'middle managers'. The job description is also a tool for coordination as it informs the employee, in written form, on the position in the structure to which he or she reports and who has authority to issue orders and/or apply rewards or sanctions.

Lateral or Horizontal Coordination

All departments or functional areas depend for functioning on other departments in the same organization. These functional areas receive inputs from other functional areas, and the quantity, quality and timeliness of these inputs are critical to their efficiency and effectiveness.

Lateral coordination is maintained through the organized delegation of responsibility to specific personnel to ensure that their counterparts receive the adequate informational inputs—advice and other resources—and take follow-up action to ensure compliance with formal rules and regulations. Lateral coordination is also maintained through the cross-referencing of records through the use of information technology. Holding regular heads-of-department meetings is a technique employed in lateral coordination.

Ad hoc Meetings

From time to time, problems involving a breakdown in coordination may occur as a result of system overload, differences in the pace of delivery of goods and services, increase in demand or any other event that can cause turbulence in the environment. Ad hoc meetings can be used as a technique to bring together all interests to discuss and find solutions to unanticipated problems.

Span of Control

This concept refers to the number of persons a manager supervises. It has been theorized that coordination is made effective by limiting the number of persons that fall within the manager's span of control. As a principle, there is no 'one best way'; there is no fixed number of persons that constitute an optimum span of control. In practice, the number will vary according to the complexity of the tasks. Tasks requiring close supervision will require smaller (or narrower) spans of control, while routine tasks will more likely require a wider span of control. Other considerations that influence the size and effectiveness of the span of control include the following:

- The ability of the managers,(ie, how many subordinates they can effectively supervise and achieve the results needed);

- The knowledge and experience of subordinates as well as their commitment to tasks. Highly committed staff with the appropriate levels of knowledge, skill and experience would require less supervision than in cases where the opposite condition exists.

- The degree of risk involved in the work situation, and consequently the amount of close supervision that is required.

Challenges to Coordination

In bureaucratic organizations, rules and regulations and standard operating procedures may be sufficient to achieve coordination. In other types of organizations, especially those where individual creativity is acceptable, as well as in some cultural environments, other factors, such as the following, may be necessary to achieve coordination of activities:

- An effective system of communication between component parts
- The commitment of groups and individuals to goals of the organization
- General knowledge of the policies, goals and objectives of the organization

As an organization becomes more decentralized, the need for coordination increases, while the process of coordination becomes more challenging. Managers at all levels need to be aware of the importance of coordination as an element in the management process.

Skills Required to Perform the Organizing Function

In order to be efficient and effective, a manager who is performing the organizing function must have skills and competencies in the following tasks:

- Identifying and preparing an inventory of all the activities that are required to get the job done. An incomplete inventory of these activities will result in deficiencies in the structure and, consequently, ineffective implementation of the plan.

- Grouping the activities according to their specialized functions within the organization. This process of dividing activities into specialized areas in large organizations is referred to as 'departmentalization'.

- Designate the relationships of authority, responsibility and accountability between persons and groups in the organization.

- Prepare an organization chart that shows, in diagrammatic format, the system of formal relationships.

- Prepare job descriptions indicating job levels and job content, including duties and responsibilities, training skills required, working conditions and economic aspects (eg, salary and benefits).

- Set out job specifications (ie, define the type of individuals who are suitable for the job, their abilities, experience, personality and educational background).

Staffing

Staffing is the element of the organising function that is concerned with providing the organization with the human resources necessary for the effective and efficient achievement of the organization's goals. This is the aspect of the organizing function in which the manager seeks to fit individuals into the structure, to ensure that the "right person is in the right place" and that good worker/organization relations are maintained throughout the period of employment.

Staffing involves several activities for which specialized education and training courses in human resources management have been developed. This training provides the managers that perform these functions with the requisite skills and competencies to do their job. In general, the manager who has responsibility for staffing should be competent in all or some of the following areas (depending on his or her job description):

- Identifying and making an inventory of the staffing needs of the organization

- Developing job descriptions and job specifications

- Conducting job interviews

- Identifying and recruiting the best person for the job

- Identifying training needs and providing training and re-training for staff

- Re-deploying staff when and where necessary

- Appraising and evaluating the job performance of employees

- Promoting and /or recommending staff for promotion

- Exercising a comprehensive knowledge of relevant industrial relations laws

- Conducting exit interviews and preparing employees for leaving the organization

Summary and Conclusions

Organizing is an ongoing process within the functions of management. Many of the organizing principles developed by the early theorists (which were considered to be universally applicable) have been revised. The structuralist approach to organizing, such as was described by Weber, has long been criticized for its rigidity and lack of allowance for creativity. Given the dynamic nature of the environment and changes in scope and content of all types of organizations, many general organizing principles and techniques have become obsolete. For example, many organizations are no longer located in one place and the concepts of departments are variably interpreted.

However, even organizations that are part of large multinational corporations require a structure within which to operate. As the decentralization of management activities increases, the need for coordination of activities becomes more important. In discriminating between theory and techniques, and in choosing between obsolete and more appropriate approaches to management, the manager should apply critical thinking and search for best fits.

Informal Organizations

No discussion of the structures and functions of the formal origination would be complete without giving some consideration to the informal organization.

Informal organizations, sometimes referred to as work groups, are defined as follows:

> Those patterned relationships which emerge spontaneously within the formal organization. The nature and practice of the informal organization are not determined by management and the complex network of inter-relationships are not shown on the organization chart. Yet they are an integral part of the formal organization and are interwoven in the very fabric of the structure of the organization.

The existence of informal groups and their effects on formal organization was first identified by the Hawthorne researchers in the 1930s. Since then, extensive studies have been carried out on the features and methods of operation of groups, mainly as a social phenomenon. It is, important, however, to study them within the context of formal organizations. One of the conclusions drawn from the Hawthorne studies was that:

> "No collection of people can be in contact for any length of time without informal groupings arising."

Informal organizations are formed as people working and interacting together in small face-to-face or primary groups develop friendships and solidarity. When these groups are established, a dynamic self-generating process occurs. As interactions between individuals increase, there is a buildup of solidarity between groups' members, which in turn becomes the basis for other types of activities that are not job-related. Typical examples of these activities include special arrangements for lunching together, shopping or even 'job trading'.

The dynamic relationship that develops, transforms the group into more than a collection of people. They develop features that are similar to those of a formal organization but are different because of the nonrational basis for their development.

Features of the Informal Organization

Informal organizations have five typical features, which can also be found in the formal organization:

1. leadership
2. standards and behavior
3. attitudes and values
4. status system
5. system of sanctions

Leadership

Every group has its leader or leaders. These leaders have a special status position and may emerge for different reasons. The leader (without even knowing it) can affect the performance of the group. However, being situational, the position can change momentarily and shift from one person to another, as the situation changes or the occasion arises.

The informal leader must embody the values of the primary group to be able to articulate the feelings of the group and be willing and able to verbalize group sentiments outside the group.

Standards of Behavior

As in the formal organization, the informal organization sets standards of behavior to which conformity is a requirement for continued membership. The standards exist for different purposes, such as the following:

- To make life more pleasant for group members, for example, through sharing a sports activity.

- To ease job pressure or help improve workmanship (eg, by helping out one another in a different situation).

- To protect the members from outside threat, real or imagined.

Attitudes and Values

The members of informal organizations, such as any professional or special-interest groups, have their own standards regarding appropriate attitudes and values. Some are without basis and are sometimes myths based on fears or wishes of the group. Some groups might have attitudes about their importance to the organization or their status position vis-à-vis other groups.

Status System

There is a status system or hierarchy within the informal organization, which might be assigned on the same basis as within the formal organization. For example, status to individuals might be assigned based on job title, pay differentiation, perhaps even dress. The acknowledgement of these status symbols must be earned by the individual, or they will be ignored by the group. In fact, in the informal organization a higher status ranking may be given to someone who is of a lower rank within the context of the formal organization. Evidence of this is demonstrated by the use of informal titles such as chief, boss, expert, etc.

Other attributes and characteristics brought into the organization may be the basis for ascribing status, depending on cultural norms. These may be age, gender, education, ethnic or racial background or physical attributes, such as height or colour.

System of Sanctions

Like the formal organization, the informal organization has a system of sanctions that is applied to those who do not conform to the accepted standards of behavior. They are also applied to individuals who articulate values and attitudes that differ from group standards. Common forms of sanctions include ostracism and expulsion from group activities. They can even manifest in physical violence, as was identified in the Bank Wiring Group of the Hawthorne studies.

Functions of the Informal Organization

The informal organization provides various functions or purposes for its members. It can provide

- companionship among its members,
- a sense of belonging,
- solutions to work problems,
- avenues for the socialization of members into the organization's culture, and
- protection for its members

Providing companionships is a very important function or purpose of the informal organization. Individuals need to be more than just another unit of labour. In informal groups, members are free to express their feelings and can satisfy their need to be with their own special group. The findings of Elton Mayo in the textile plant showed that persons who worked in isolation failed to meet production standards. When the pattern of work was changed to allow for social interaction, production improved.

In addition to providing friendship, the group provides a sense of belonging, identification and understanding from others. Human beings need acceptance and the natural gregariousness of spirit needs to be satisfied through bonding with others in a group.

Another critical purpose of the informal organization is that it helps provide solutions to work problems. Where there might be reluctance to seek assistance from the supervisor or boss, other group members can provide useful guidance where members might feel a greater sense of security.

The socialization of members is another important function, especially where new employees need to be socialized into the norms of the organization. Often, the role of guiding the new members into accepted standards of behavior can be effectively done only through the informal organization. Orientation programmes that are part of the processes of the formal organization tend not to be done as comprehensively and effectively. Many of the subtleties of the culture are often ignored or are too complex to be adequately addressed in the typical orientation, or they are avoided by the formal leaders.

Frequently, members of the informal organization need to be protected from outside pressure and excessive use of authority. The group may decide to resist, for example, management's demands for higher outputs or attempts to provide lower benefits or to introduce what they consider to be unreasonable changes in routines. By using its strength of numbers, the informal group can resist these pressures and can cause changes in management policy.

Effects on the Formal Organization

The informal organization can have a positive as well as a negative effect on the formal organization, as follows:

- By providing satisfaction for the social needs of the individual, it can increase motivation, prevent excessive absenteeism and reduce staff turnover. Thus, it supports stability of tenure.

- The informal organization provides a useful channel of communication. By identifying and working through the informal leader, management can be informed of the sentiments of groups, thereby permitting an easier flow of upward and downward communication.

- The informal organization can actually perform a supervisory role; an informal leader may be the channel through which orders and instructions are translated into terms more familiar to group members.

- The informal organization can reinterpret managerial orders that are not in the best interest of the formal organization. This occurs when decisions are made by managers who are far away from the production activities and unable to envision the possibilities or problems that arise from unrealistic directives.

- The informal organization can provide an atmosphere more conducive to stimulating creativity and developing new ideas in situations when conflicts and/or problems arise between the formal organization and informal groupings.

- The informal organization can work at cross-purposes with the formal one when the goals and interests of each are different. Conflicts between the requirements of the employer and needs of the group can and do lead to sabotage, among other undesirable workplace situations. However, these conflicts can be catalysts for change within the formal organization.

Conclusion

Management cannot prevent the growth of informal organizations. The successful administrator will seek to use the informal relationships among subordinates to develop a structure of communication and establish an atmosphere of trust. Groups differ according to the basis of their cohesiveness. Therefore, it is important that managers study and understand groups, and the factors that influence their effectiveness, and integrate their findings into the management process.

References

Cole, G.A (2003) *Management: Theory & Practice* op cit., chap. 21, 22 (Cenage Learning, London).

Hampton, David (1977) "Organizing", in *Contemporary Management*, op cit. pp. 260-275 (McGraw-Hill, New York).

Hampton, David: (1977) "Coordination, Authority and Power", in *Contemporary Management*, op. cit. pp. 282-312 (McGraw-Hill, New York).

Robbins, Stephen R. & Coulter Mary (2004) "Organizational Structure and Design", in *Management*, op cit. chap. 10, pp. 299-334 (Prentice-Hall, London).

Straus, George & Sayles, Leonard R (1980) "Organization Design Alternative Structure", in *Personnel: The Human Problems of Management* 4th ed., chap. 14 (Prentice Hall, New York).

Online Resources

Mote, Dave. Organizational Theory. In Reference for Business: Encyclopedia of Business, 2nd ed., http://www.referenceforbusiness.com/encyclopedia/Oli-Per/Organization-Theory.html

Bakan I, Tasliyan, M, and Eraslan, I. The Effect of Technology on Organizational Behaviour and the Nature of Work., http://www.iamot.org/conference/index.php/ocs/4/paper/viewFile/644/141

Informal Organizational Structure: The Hawthorne Studies, http://www.analytictech.com/mb021/Hawthorne.html

RSA Animate - Drive: The surprising truth about what motivates us, http://www.youtube.com/watch?v=u6XAPnuFjJc

Directing

Introduction

In many respects, the directing function is more complex than the two management functions previously discussed. Whereas planning and organizing involve the application of technical and conceptual skills, directing requires the effective use of human relations skills. In general, directing involves issuing orders and assigning tasks to subordinates, to ensure that 'directives' are carried out in the interest of the achievement of organization goals within the structure of the organization.

Directing is the management function that was first referred to by the French theorist Henri Fayol as 'commanding'. He stated that "the objective of every manager is to get the optimum return from all the employees of his unit in the interest of the entire organization". Sometime later Luther Gulick, another classical theorist, defined the function as 'directing'.

In performing the directing functions, the manager applies the use of such human relations skills as leadership, communication, motivation, delegation and the effective use of formal authority. Developing skills and competencies in the performance of the functions is critical to the effective management of human resources.

Theoretical Approaches to Directing

In the discussion on the theoretical perspectives, it was observed that the assumptions or generalizations that managers make about human nature determine the way in which they perform the directing function. Thus, managerial approaches fall within different theoretical frameworks.

Classical Theorists

The traditional managers (who Douglas McGregor refers to as Theory X managers) hold assumptions about people that lead them to use certain strategies for managerial control. The scientific manager and the purely bureaucratic manager emphasize rules and regulations and the 'carrot and stick' approach to motivating people.

Human Relations Theorists

The human relations managers, referred to as Theory Y managers, make more provision for self-direction and participation. This 'management by objectives', for example, makes allowance for the subordinate to use his or her ingenuity and creativity. Theory Y managers make assumptions that people in organizations have the capacity to assume responsibility and make decisions. Therefore, they do not have to be controlled or coerced to perform tasks in the interest of the organization.

Systems and Contingency Approaches

This theoretical approach makes provision for more flexibility in the selection of a style of directing and, consequently, is more inclusive of the previous approaches. It incorporates the view that there is no one best way to perform the directing function.

Elements of the Directing Function

The directing function includes several discrete elements that a manager is to understand to develop specialized skills in order to effectively perform the function. The primary element that a manager needs in order to direct people in a formal organization is 'authority'. This was discussed in Weber's theoretical concept of the bureaucracy.

Authority

In formal organizations, the directing function is performed by persons who hold formal positions and who have been given formal authority. However, the ability to exercise authority is not a given.

'Authority' has been defined as "the capacity to evoke compliance in others on the basis of formal position or any other psychological inducements, rewards or sanctions that may accompany the formal position".

This definition leads to the conclusion that authority in the organization flows naturally from the hierarchical position that a person holds. In the rational-legal sense, the essential feature of authority is that there is a special official relationship in which those giving the orders believe they have a right to do so and those receiving the orders believe that they have a duty to obey.

These views on authority were questioned by neo-classicist Chester Bernard, who developed an acceptance theory of authority, and stated four bases on which a given order may be accepted or resisted by a subordinate. In rational-legal systems (ie, formal organizations) there are different beliefs into which individuals or groups have been socialized; and these beliefs, separately or in combination, determine the extent to which formal authority is legitimated (or accepted) by subordinates.

Bases of Legitimation

Formal Role (Position)

This is the most commonly accepted basis of legitimation. Formal letters of appointment usually state who holds authority (ie, who reports to whom, and who is responsible for what). The formal position that a superior holds is supported by certain structural, physical and psychological factors. These are as follows:

The structural factors, which include the superior's access to and control over information. The structure of the organization places certain limits on the amount of information available to subordinates. This results in the centralization of initiative and restriction of access to centres of decision making. The structure also has the in-built power given to superiors to apply sanctions (penalties) or give rewards.

Physical factors, which may include the distance between the office of management and the location or workplace of the subordinate. Even in the same building, this distance might be marked by the size of the door at the entrance to the boss's office. In some instances, mannerisms (eg, body language) of some officials are physical factors that require subordinates to act in a particular way in their presence.

Psychological factors, such as manner of dress, are also symbols of authority. In some organizations, this is marked by distinctions in colour, style and other symbols (eg, the uniform worn by officers of different ranks in an army.) These symbols indicate the status of the individual and these can function to legitimate the individual's authority.

Expertise

A second basis on which authority is commonly legitimated is the superior knowledge and technical competence possessed by an official. This legitimating factor tends to be more widely accepted in societies in which the knowledge base of employees has been broadened. The more qualified the rank and file employees become, the less likely they are to accept the orders of persons whom they believe are not qualified to issue those orders. The expertise factor suggests that the manager who rises to the top position purely on the basis of seniority, without adequate educational/professional qualifications to hold the formal position, will have difficulty in getting his or her authority legitimated.

Rapport

A third legitimating factor, rapport, has its base in the human relations aspect of the organization. Rapport can act in competition with, or complementary to, the previously mentioned factors. The manager who holds positional authority can have his or her authority more effectively legitimated by conducting official functions with a 'human touch'. In democratic societies where egalitarianism is considered a valued concept, rapport develops as a norm for interpersonal relationships. This is so even where structures are established on authoritarian principles, such as in a bureaucracy.

Furthermore, possession of expertise is not considered to be a sufficient condition for ignoring the feelings and attitudes of subordinates. Research has shown that the power to exercise authority is positively related to affection for the person exercising it.

Generalized Deference to Authority

This is a broad category of basis for legitimacy that flows from culture and customs. In some societies, respect for authority is the socially accepted pattern of behavior. The organization can benefit from these societal norms into which individuals are socialized, beginning from infancy, and which follow through the various stages of the individual's development. The child is taught deference to parents, teachers, and religious leaders, and this carries through to influence behavior in the organization.

The Purpose of the Organization

In some instances, authority may be accepted if the subordinate believes in, and identifies with, the purpose of the organization and is confident that a command is in keeping with that purpose. In other words, if the orders issued appear to be compatible with the subordinate's understanding of the mission or purpose of the organization, there is a strong possibility that the legitimacy of that order will be established.

Avoidance of Responsibility

The unwillingness or disinclination of some individuals to assume responsibility may provide a basis for authority to be legitimated. It is not unusual for persons to carry out assigned tasks without question, rather than having to use their initiative or to make decisions. Sometimes, individuals prefer to be told what to do and to let someone else take the responsibility for the outcome, particularly if the task is not regarded as pleasant.

Personality (Physical and Psychological) Traits

Physical and psychological traits are another common basis on which authority is legitimated. In some situations, the view is held that some types of persons are destined to lead and others are destined to follow. Several personality traits fall into this system of beliefs, which also includes social class, race and colour. If the superior's leadership style fits the subordinate's perception of what is acceptable leadership behavior, this will create a legitimating condition. In some societies, certain professional groups are also given a social mandate to exercise authority. These may include doctors, lawyers and the rich and famous. Consequently, their authority is legitimated without question. Sometimes physical features (eg, tall, dark and handsome) may also be legitimating factors.

Although these bases for legitimating authority have been discussed separately, it will be obvious that there will be different combinations of these bases in every situation. Formal position may be combined with expertise and sometimes there is conflict between the two bases. The formal head who is a generalist might resent the specialist who has authority on the basis of expertise. However, this conflict may be resolved through good rapport. While some may act on the basis of deference to authority because of socialization, this can change when persons become better qualified, academically or professionally.

Limitations to Authority

In the same way that authority can be legitimated, subordinates also have the power to put limits on a manager's authority. These powers may be exercised in the following different ways:

Disobedience

An officer may choose to openly defy the order given. This is a course of action open to any person who is employed on a free, contractual basis. This would create a problem for the manager who would be faced with the decision of either withdrawing the order (thus undermining his or her own authority) or taking disciplinary action against the subordinate, as prescribed in the rules. Both courses of action can have serious negative implications for future relationships.

Forming Staff Associations

Groups within an organization may formalize their association in order to be better able to put pressure on management and to resist their authority in the areas of working conditions, salaries and benefits. Their ability to invoke the strike weapon is one way of putting limits on official authority.

Nonconfrontational Resistance

There are ways in which subordinates resist authority without confrontation. They can go through the motions of compliance without accomplishing any objective, or claim to have forgotten an instruction or to have misinterpreted the directives. These acts are extremely difficult to monitor and can serve to frustrate the manager.

Work to Rule

This form of resistance is also difficult to manage. While the rules exist to guide the actions of officers, overzealous observance of rules can work against the achievement of the organization's goals, as many of the important day-to-day activities are not prescribed in the rules. This form of resistance has been known to negatively affect an organization's effectiveness.

The Use of Authority

In light of the foregoing, the manager must seek to develop a balance between his or her capacity to use authority and the subordinate's capacity to resist that authority. This can be achieved through an understanding of the environment, the people and the tasks and applying a contingency approach that will provide the most appropriate mixture of suggestion, persuasion and discussion as agents for influencing the behavior of subordinates.

Leadership

Definition

Leadership as a theoretical construct has been researched and studied exclusively for decades, and several authoritative books and articles have been written on the subject. The term 'leadership' has been used in many different situations and with a wide variety of interpretations.

Leadership has been defined as a status position held by a person in a formal or informal situation. It has also been defined as a process that, when applied in the organizational context, involves "the process of influencing the activities of an organized group in its effort towards goal setting and goal achievement. In essence, the leader is the person who assists members of a group that is pursuing the same purpose to direct their energies towards the achievement of group-related objectives.

In formal organizations, the leader is the person who holds legitimate power, based on the nature and scope of his or her formal position. This power is legitimated by the belief of the followers (subordinates) in the rightness of the rules by which the organization is governed.

Effective Leadership

One of the major responsibilities of a manager who is performing the directing function is to be effective as a leader. Up to the 1940s, there was a strongly held view that the ability to lead was a characteristic of some people, which others did not have. The leader was considered to be someone blessed with certain qualities that were inherited and made it relatively easy for him or her to lead. This view was referred to as the 'trait approach'. Some writers even prepared a list of leadership qualities, which included the following:

- Intelligence and good judgement
- Insight and imagination
- The ability to accept responsibility

- A sense of humour
- A well-balanced personality
- A sense of justice

After the 1940s, the trait approach was abandoned and replaced by the situational approach. Empirical research has shown that some of the most famous world leaders had personalities that were the exact opposite of those listed in the trait approach. The view developed in the situational approach is that leadership is a function of personality and the social system in dynamic interaction. It is a contingency approach to leadership that says that there is no one best way of leading: different kinds of situations or organizational circumstances require different kinds of leadership, and the traits of the successful leader are dependent, to a large extent, on a particular situation.

In order to be an effective leader, a manager must choose from among several alternative styles of leadership behavior. A leader may choose a style that is directive, authoritarian and concerned mainly with getting the job done. There is hardly any concern for people, except as 'factors of production'. This leader is 'task-centred', which was described by Douglas McGregor as the Theory X leader/manager. Another style of leadership behavior is referred to as 'people-centred', which is a more democratic style and allows for participation of followers at all levels of decision-making. This style falls more easily into the category that McGregor refers to as Theory Y leadership style.

The 'situational' or 'contingency' approach to leadership suggests, however, that the effective leader will not be totally task-centred or people-centred, but will choose a leadership behavior that falls on a continuum between the two styles.

Warren H. Schmidt, business expert, identifies five typical styles of leadership behavior from which a manager may choose, ranging on a continuum from highly 'leadership-centred' to highly 'group-centred'. The styles are as follows:

1. **Telling**—the leader tells the followers what to do.

2. **Persuading**—the followers accept the decision that has already been made.

3. **Consulting**—the leader consults with the followers to arrive at a decision, but reserves the right to select the best alternatives.

4. **Joining**—the leader joins the group in decision-making and accepts the decision of the majority.

5. **Delegating**—the leader delegates responsibility to the group to find a solution to a situation or problem within the formal boundaries that have been set.

Selecting a Leadership Style

Taking into consideration the dynamic interaction between leaders, followers and the social system in which they operate, it is important that all the forces in these elements be carefully considered when selecting a leadership style. These are as follows:

- The forces in the leader
- The forces in the group
- The forces in the situation

Forces in the Leader

The criticism of the trait approach to leadership does not suggest that a leader leaves his personality out of the process. Consideration must also be given to his own feeling in a given decision-making situation. The following forces will also influence his or her leadership behaviors:

- The leader's value system
- The level of confidence that he or she has in the group
- His or her own leadership inclinations
- His or her feelings of security in uncertain situations

These highly personal variables make up the forces that influence the leader's behavior and should be carefully analysed when he or she decides which behavior to choose.

Forces in the Group Members

There is an axiom that "there can be no leader without followers". When selecting a leadership behavior the forces in the group also have to be considered. These forces should include—

- the employees' knowledge and experience;
- their interest in the problem;
- their readiness for responsibilities;
- their expectations about their leader;
- their understanding of the goals of the organization; and
- their individual personality variables.

The existence of these forces will have either positive or negative elements, which should influence the leader in making a decision about the use of his or her leadership authority in the group.

Forces in the Situation

The situational or contingency approach to management is important when considering a leadership behavior. In addition to personal and group forces, understanding forces in the situation is critical to the process. The forces include the values and traditions that are part of the organization's personality, and these will influence the behavior of people who work in them. The size of the organization, the type of activities in which it is involved and the constraints to which its operations are subjected (eg, constraints of time, availability of resources) all contribute to the organizational environment and can determine the best fit for a leadership style and behavior.

If leadership is to be effective, none of these forces should be allowed to predominate in the selection of a particular behavior. An effective leader must be able to accurately assess the factors that are influencing a situation, as well as the capabilities and needs of the followers.

Characteristics of the Effective Leader

Based on research over time, a number of important leadership characteristics have been identified. A good leader is said to have the following characteristics:

- Believes in the aims of the organization
- Is intelligent
- Has a facility for making decisions
- Possesses good communication skills, including listening skills
- Demonstrates sensitivity and insight
- Possesses a willingness to lead
- Has a sound knowledge of the group and its members
- Has self-confidence
- Has a sound knowledge of the overall tasks and what needs to be done
- Is able to delegate effectively
- Is consistent
- Is always a good example to followers

While these are generalized concepts, they can provide a leader with useful tools in selecting a leadership behavior.

Communication

Introduction

Communication is defined as the process of creating, transmitting and interpreting ideas, facts, opinions and feelings between two or more people. Communication is a critical element in the directing function. It is through this process that a manager does the following:

- Exercises authority through the issuing of orders
- Provides leadership by influencing the actions of others
- Motivates staff by releasing their potential to contribute to organizational goals
- Delegates responsibility

Communication provides the link between the other functions of management. It establishes unity and coherence throughout the organization and between organizations.

Direction or Flow of Communication

Organizational communication flows in different directions, each having its own purpose and requiring a different set of techniques. The flow might be either—

- vertical (ie, downwards and upwards) or
- horizontal (lateral)

Vertical Communication

Downward communication is the direction in which those in positions of authority communicate policies, plans and decisions and issue orders through the organization's chain of command. This traditional flow of communication usually is followed in mechanistic organizations (eg, a bureaucracy). The size of the organization determines the number of levels through which the communication passes and its effectiveness can be limited if the flow is in only one direction.

Upward communication includes the ideas, suggestions, comments and complaints of employees. The process is usually determined by the organization's rules and regulations for joint consultations and grievance procedures. Upward communication also flows through direct representations from work groups. It is one of the means through which human relations problems are addressed.

Horizontal or Lateral Communication

This is communication that flows between persons on the same level (rank) in the organization or between persons who do not have a supervisor-subordinate relationship with one another. This flow usually occurs between people in different departments and units in the same organization to provide support information or to request support in the performance of some specific task.

Lateral communication is necessary for the coordination and integration of efforts. Provision for this flow is integral to the organizing function to ensure rationality among the diverse operations of complex organizations. Lateral communication is generally used to provide task-oriented or technical information.

Medium of Communication

Managers in large organizations communicate with a wide variety of persons who occupy different positions within the system. Because of the volume and diversity of information to be transmitted, a manager must have knowledge and skills in developing and managing an effective system of communication.

In formal organizations, messages are communicated through different media or channels. Skills in the use of these media are essential to being an effective manager.

Oral Communication

This is the most commonly used method in organizations—whether large or small. A wide range of activities are carried out through this medium. They include face-to-face meetings and discussions individually or in large or small groups. Oral communication facilitates speedy transmission and easy clarification of thoughts and ideas and avoidance of misunderstanding. However, it lacks the security of permanence in recording and recall.

Written Communication

Written communication is the form that was recommended for use in bureaucratic organizations. This medium includes letters and memoranda, reports, newsletters, circulars and the like. Increased use is being made of all forms of electronic media for transmitting written communication, especially e-mail. This prevalence of electronic media has revolutionized the communication process. However, some forms of electronic media, such as tweeting and texting, are not universally acceptable, due to the danger of tampering and altering and misunderstanding context.

Telephone Communication

This is the most rapid means of communication and has become the most widely used medium, especially since the cellular phone revolution. However, this medium does not allow for non-verbal responses and can also present difficulties in interpreting nuances of personal accents (speech). Persons with hearing impairment may have problems with this medium. Formal requirement for back-up written communication has always been considered necessary for permanence in recording.

The pros and cons of each of these media must be considered by managers when selecting one or a combination of media. In face-to-face (oral) situations, for example, nonverbal actions (referred to as 'body language') often accompany spoken words. The manager should be careful not to inadvertently send nonverbal messages that might be misinterpreted by their receivers.

Techniques for Effective Communication

Effective communication does not take place automatically. Knowing 'how' to communicate is as important as knowing 'what' to communicate. Regardless of the medium used, there are specific elements in the process that contribute to effectiveness in communication. The elements include the following:

The idea/message

The idea that is to be communicated should be a well-conceived one. If the idea is not well thought out, the process will not be effective. A manager must ensure that pressure to develop an idea does not compromise the effort to clarify the idea.

The organization

The organization of the message is vital to its effectiveness. The message must be so organized to ensure that it is a true reflection of the idea that is to be communicated.

The transmission

The transmission of the message is very important to the process. Transmission moves the idea towards its destination. The sender should be careful not to send too many ideas at the same time, or to include unnecessary information, as this could undermine the process. When transmitting orally (face to face), the sender should avoid the use of distracting nonverbal action.

Reception

The reception of the message links the sender with the receiver. Communication can only be effective if it is received by the person(s) for whom it is intended. Every effort should be made to avoid interruptions ('noise'), or any distractions that could block the reception. Communication should take place at the right time and in the right place to facilitate reception.

Understanding/Interpretation

The message must be understood by the reviewer in the same way that it is intended by the sender. While the manager does not have full control over this aspect of the process, he or she should be careful to avoid the use of jargon, especially when communicating with others outside of the particular discipline or area of specialization.

Action

The action that should follow the sending of the message is the required feedback. Communication is not completed until this objective has been achieved. If there is no action, the sender of a message has no way of knowing if the message was received and understood. A manager should set some specific time frame in which to receive this feedback. Failure to do this could contribute to ineffective communication.

Communication Barriers

All organizations experience some problems with their communication system. Many industrial relations problems are related to failure in communication between managers and employees. Managers who have responsibility for the directing function should be aware of the factors that are barriers to effective communication and know how to manage them. Barriers to effective communication include the following:

The Human Element

One of the most difficult problems in communication is dealing with the human element. Human beings have difficulty understanding one another, because of the differences in their backgrounds, culture, knowledge and attitudes. This is a pervasive and often irreconcilable problem in all types of organizations.

Size and Complexity

The size and complexity of modern organizations is a major cause of problems. The volume of information that has to be transmitted and the large number of persons who need to receive information make it difficult for communication to flow freely.

Content

The diverse nature of the information that has to be communicated may also contribute to problems. With increases in specialization and departmentalization of tasks, communication needs become more diverse and discrete and require more careful management.

Physical Barriers

These are related to the physical structure of formal organizations, which prevents access between senders and receivers.

Psychological Barriers

There are psychological problems related to the filtering of information, in which individuals hear only what they want to hear, or take from the information what fits their own preconceived ideas. This distortion of information, in which the meaning of words may be deliberately changed or misinterpreted, can be a barrier to effective communication.

Managing Communication Barriers

Being aware of these barriers is a first step to being able to manage communication—one of the more difficult tasks that a manager will have. Some steps that a manager should take to manage these problems include the following:

- Carefully follow the steps in the communication process and protocol

- Develop skills in writing and speaking

- Improve listening skills and provide feedback to messages received

- Make every effort to reduce the physical barriers that are part of the organizational structure, to allow for upward communication

- Seek to create an environment of trust in an attempt to reduce the psychological barriers

Summary

Communication is the process of passing information between persons. It is the key to unlocking the directing function. Organizations use different modes of communication, all of which have either a positive or negative impact on effectiveness.

There are techniques that a manager can use in order to be an effective communicator. At the same time, there are barriers or problems that he or she will encounter in the process. Being aware of these problems is a first step towards developing skills and techniques in overcoming them.

Delegation

Introduction

Delegation is the process by which a manager transfers a part of his or her legitimate authority to a subordinate but retains the ultimate responsibility that has been assigned to the formal position. Because managers are unable to personally accomplish all the tasks in any given job situation, they must seek the assistance of others who are assigned to them as part of the organization's resources. However, the manager will always have to be involved in the process of guiding the actions of subordinates towards the achievement of the organization's objectives.

In order to delegate effectively, a manager should know 'why' he or she should delegate, 'when' to delegate, and 'how' to delegate.

Reasons to Delegate

It is important for a manager to understand the purpose of delegation. Both managers and their subordinates must be committed to the process, and they must agree on the objectives to be achieved. It is important, for example, that the subordinate should not interpret delegation as the manager's attempt at 'passing the buck'. The following are some important reasons why a manager should delegate:

- By giving some of the less important operational tasks to the subordinate, the manager will be left with more time to concentrate on the strategic activities, such as decision-making and planning and interpreting and communicating policies to subordinates.

- Delegation helps to speed up decision-making and implementation in routine matters. Those on the front line who have access to information that they can use to make urgent decisions should be given the authority to use such information.

- Giving responsibility for tasks that are in the scope of their competence will enhance the growth and development of subordinates (job enrichment).

- Delegation is an important method of providing an environment for creativity and development of problem-solving techniques at the lower levels of the organization.

These reasons for delegation are compatible with the Theory Y approach to management and motivation. By delegating tasks to subordinates, a manager can help to satisfy the social, ego and esteem needs of employees and facilitate the process of "getting things done through people".

When to Delegate

Although delegation can serve to satisfy the needs of both managers and subordinates, it is not always appropriate for a manager to delegate. The following are some guidelines that should be followed when deciding if and when to delegate:

- A manager should delegate when someone else has more technical knowledge, skill or experience and is, therefore, able to do a better job.

- Delegating a task to someone who is adequately qualified will leave the manager with more time to do other tasks. Even when the quality of output might not be at optimum level, it should be delegated, as long as it would not be a threat to effectiveness.

- Delegation could be used as a means of providing subordinates with the training that would not be available otherwise.

- If someone else has more time available or is able to do a comparable job at a lower cost, then the tasks should be delegated to that person.

Barriers to Delegation

In addition to having knowledge of why and when to delegate, a manager has to understand that a desire to delegate is not sufficient condition to be able to carry out that function. Managers should know that there are some real obstacles or barriers to effective delegation. These may be either organizational or personal barriers.

Organizational Barriers

These are barriers that are related to the organizational environment, such as the structure, the tasks and the people or the culture. For example:

- Sometimes in large functional organizations, subordinates may not have the authority to get the cooperation of other departments, thus requiring the senior official to take responsibility to get the requested support to complete a task.

- Sometimes the pressure on a manager to meet deadlines in completing important tasks may become a barrier to delegating, as a manager may feel that there is no time to delegate.

- In situations of frequent crisis, such as in turbulent environments where changes occur regularly, the need to make non-programmed decisions can be a barrier to delegation to employees at lower levels of the organization.

- In high-risk situations where the outcome of the action might cause a serious setback to the operations of the organization, there might be reluctance on the part of the manager to delegate, as well as on the part of the subordinate to accept the delegated responsibility.

Personal Barriers

Some barriers are caused by the personal feelings and attitudes of the manager. Delegation is an activity that is based on the philosophy of applying "management by objectives". The philosophy states that the manager must believe that the subordinate has the ability to be creative and to be self-motivated. In other words, delegation is an approach used by Theory Y managers. A Theory X manager would have difficulty with delegation, for a number of reasons. These barriers would have to be overcome if a manager is to delegate effectively:

- A feeling that the subordinate has less knowledge and experience and therefore would not do a good job.

- A fear that the subordinate needs close supervision and will therefore be a source of constant interruptions.

- A belief that sharing responsibility with others could result in loss of control, power or prestige.

- A common concern that, if the manager delegates, a subordinate might gain experience and knowledge and become qualified enough to take over the manager's job.

- Fear that employees will want some additional reward if they are asked to take on additional tasks, thus raising industrial dispute issues.

Techniques for Effective Delegation

It is a well-established fact that some managers do not like to assign tasks to subordinates. It has been noted that the organization's environment can create obstacles to delegation as well as the personal feelings of the manager. Another reason why managers do not delegate, and why the delegating process may not be effective when they do, is the lack of skill in delegating. The following are some guidelines for overcoming these obstacles and improving delegation skills:

- Practice being a good communicator: this is very important to effective delegating. Give clear instructions about the task that is being delegated.

- Involve staff in the planning process so that they will understand their roles in the implementation process.

- Ensure that the person to whom a task is being delegated has the basic knowledge and skills to do the job as well as commitment to the completion of the task.

- Be prepared for errors and mistakes and use criticisms constructively. Accept a subordinate's failure and use it as a learning experience, and not a reason to cause embarrassment.

- Set scheduled times for monitoring and evaluation, but keep avenues of communication open to address requests for clarification.

- Provide the subordinates with the necessary resources, such as equipment and raw materials, that are needed to carry out the task, and give them a reasonable amount of time in which to finish the job.

Delegation can only be carried out effectively in an organizational environment where there is mutual trust. The forces in the group, in particular the way the subordinates feel about their superior, will produce either a positive or negative organizational climate and will ultimately determine the effectiveness of the delegation.

Summary

Delegation is an important tool in the directing function. It can be used as a means of relieving the manager of some of the many tasks to be performed. Effectiveness in delegation can only be achieved when a manager knows the reasons for delegating. Essentially, delegation can help subordinates to grow and achieve a higher level of needs satisfaction.

There are conditions under which delegation is either appropriate or inappropriate. A manager needs to know when to delegate as well as the factors, whether personal or organizational, that can be barriers to delegation. By being aware of and developing certain techniques, a manager can improve his or her delegation skills.

Supervision

The role of the supervisor is critical to the directing function. It incorporates techniques in areas of leading, communicating, delegating and motivating staff to give maximum effort to the achievement of organizational goals.

Any person who performs the function of supervising the work of subordinates and assisting top managers in carrying out the management functions—planning, organizing, directing and controlling—is described as a 'middle manager'.

The primary function of the supervisor or middle manager is to influence productivity, to ensure that the human and material resources are organized and managed efficiently and effectively. The supervisor has the following important responsibilities:

- Correctly interpreting the main policy directives that are set out by top management and converting them into organizational goals and objectives.
- Receiving orders, instructions and information from senior management and clarifying and transmitting information to subordinates.
- Maintaining equipment by taking both preventive and corrective action.
- Ensuring that established standards of quality are maintained throughout the unit.
- Creating a good image of the organization for both employees in the organization and the general public.
- Showing concern for the morale of subordinates.
- Ensuring stability of tenure and reducing staff turnover by using good human relations skills.
- Arranging in-service training for subordinates to improve the quality of their performance.
- Showing recognition for employees' work and by so doing facilitating their motivation.
- Minimizing employees' grievances by being a good listener.
- Acting as an intermediate between subordinates and top management and between subordinates.

- Setting a good example, demonstrating excellent leadership qualities.

In order to perform the above functions effectively, the supervisor must possess the following qualities:

- Be knowledgeable about his or her staff and the strengths and weaknesses in the areas of their job requirements and personality traits.

- Have skills in leadership, communication and motivation.

- Be able to delegate effectively.

- Be familiar with the job being performed by subordinates.

- Be able to perform and give guidance in the managerial functions of planning, organizing and evaluating.

Summary

The supervisor (middle manager) performs a very complex and important role in the organization, which can be very challenging. As a front line manager, the supervisor is often seen as the 'face' of the organization, to employees within and the general public. He or she has to maintain a balance between the demands of top management and the needs of subordinates.

Despite the problems and challenges associated with the position, the supervisor has the opportunity to be an agent of change by applying a wide range of knowledge and skills to the function of directing the energies of employees towards the achievement of organizational goal.

General Conclusions

Every manager performing the directing function is required to have a wide range of skills and competencies in the management of human resources. In performing this function, the manager must be aware of the fact that there is no one best way of getting optimum return from all the employees in his unit. The manager must apply all branches of the human relations school of management thought and be willing to adapt managerial styles and behavior to the given situation, individual or group.

References

Aurner, Robert & Wolf, Morris P. (1967) "Ten Commandments of Good Communication", in *Effective Communication in Business* 5th ed., American Management Assn. (South Western Publishing Co., Ohio).

Bass, Bernard M. (1990) *Bass & Stogdill's Handbook of Leadership: Theory, Research, & Managerial Applications*, 3rd Edition, (Free Press, New York).

Brown, J.A.C.: "Leaders and Leadership" in *The Social Psychology of Industry*.

Kevin Theodore (1982, May) "How to Improve your Delegation Habits", in *Management Review*, pp. 58-61.

Luthans, Fred (1973) "Approaches to Management", in *Organizational Behaviour*, 2nd ed., chap. 3,International Student Edition (McGraw Hill, Kogakusha Ltd).

Schmidt, Warren H: "The Leader Look at Styles of Leadership".

Strauss, G. & Sayles, Leonard R. (2006, January) "Communications: The Information Transmission process", in *Management* 4th ed. op cit., chap. 8 (South Western Publishing Co., Ohio).

Online Resources

Ball, John. (2006, March) Power to the people. Management and supervision relevant to ACCA Qual. Paper F1 and CAT Paper 5, http://www.acca.co.uk/pubs/students/publications/student_accountant/archive/ball0306.pdf

Successful delegation: Using the power of other people's help. From Mind Tools, http://www.mindtools.com/pages/article/newLDR_98.htm

Controlling

Introduction

Control can be defined as a process of monitoring organizational activities to verify whether everything occurs in conformity with the plan adopted, the instructions issued and the principles established. It is the final link in the cycle of the management process, and provides the feedback into the first step in the process. Control is the final link in the cycle of the management process.

Purpose of Control in Management

The process of controlling involves such activities as reviewing, assessing, monitoring, appraising, evaluating, all of which are directed towards measuring a given situation against a standard that has been set.

Where there is no measurement there can be no control. Control activities provide information on the following:

Whether the objectives that were set out at the planning stage have been achieved, whether there are gaps (or differences) between the stated (or expected) and the actual results and the reasons, or the differences (if they exist).

Whether the 'structures' (human and material resources) are adequate for the tasks to be performed, including whether too few or too many persons have been assigned to the activities as well as their levels of capabilities.

The appropriateness of the 'directing' approaches, leadership styles, methods of communication and delegation.

The action necessary to correct any deviation between the plan and the outcome.

Types of Control

Control action can be taken at different stages in an activity. There are three types of control, which are represented by the timeframes in which each takes place.

Feed forward control

This is a preventive method of controlling that relies mainly on reports of friends and is intended to prevent an anticipated problem. However, the accuracy and timeliness of the information used in this type of control is often very difficult to obtain and could be misleading.

Concurrent control

This type of control takes place during the use of constant monitoring and close supervision to avert problems or correct deviations from the plan on a timely basis. This is a type of control that can be achieved through the use of technical mechanisms, such as word processors, to identity problems as soon as they occur and so avoid the long delays in taking corrective action.

Feedback control

This is the most widely used type of control. It takes place on completion of an activity and allows time for collation or relevant reports and data collection. While some controls, such as reviews of financial reports, can only be done through the feedback type of control, a real problem lies in the fact that time is lost in identifying problems. It is often different and sometimes impossible to correct deviations.

Depending on the situation, a manager might choose to combine more than one type of control in order to achieve the highest level of effectiveness.

Elements Necessary for Effective Control

In the process of effectively controlling the management of any organization, the following elements must be included:

- There must be an established 'plan of action' with clearly defined goals and objectives. The most important purpose of the control system is to ensure that the goals and objectives that have been set are being achieved, and that the 'route' being taken towards achievement is in tandem with the plan.

- There is an identifiable 'human organization' in place to carry out the plans. This may be summarized through existing organization charts, job descriptions, job specifications, etc., and individual authority and responsibility are clearly stated and understood by all.

- The principles and guidelines for 'directing' personnel activities, the rules of discipline and expectations for equity, rewards and sanctions are in keeping with accepted standards.

- That structure is maintained for 'coordinating' activities between individuals, groups and departments as well as other stakeholders.

- There must be an organized system for collecting, collating, classifying, storing and retrieving information and for communicating relevant data to the right person in the right form at the right time.

The effective measuring of performance of persons and/or activities requires adherence to certain principles.

Uniformity of Standards

In control, the standard for measuring output must be consistent with the standard stated in the plan. If, for example, planning objectives are stated in weight, height or money value, these standards must be used in the control process.

Timelines of Reporting

The information used for measuring performance must be collected on time. These time frames must be stated in the plan and structures put in place to ensure that information is collected in time, according to its usefulness in the management process. Relevant information should be sent to the right person at the right time.

Timeliness will vary according to the need for information – from the daily audit of a petty cash account to an hourly monitoring of the effect of a drug administered to a patient, to monthly, quarterly, annual reports, etc.

Accuracy in Reporting

The measurement system should include the criteria for accuracy. The level of accuracy that is desired will depend on the situation; and where variations in accuracy can be tolerated, this should be clearly stated at the time of the establishment of a control system.

Feedback Mechanism

The source of feedback used in control is critical to the system of information gathering. Formal feedback includes written reports and statistical reports. Informal feedback may include rumor, gossip and unofficial discussions both internal and external to the organization.

Personal experience may also be a useful source of information (eg, intuition, judgement). These sources require careful scrutiny and application of management skills to ensure effectiveness in their use.

Control Techniques

One of the main purposes of a control system in management is to compare performance against set targets. In Fayol's definition, this function is "to verify whether everything occurs in conformity with the plan". Control techniques include the following:

Comparing 'Planned' and 'Actual' Results

There are several techniques or methods used for presenting 'actual' and 'projected' results, which allow for easy analysis. These include bar charts, pie charts, Gantt charts, etc. There are also mathematical equations that can show ratios between 'actual' and 'planned' results and programmes exist that can produce comparative results in a very short time.

Regardless of the methods used, the information presented is only an indicator of what has occurred or is occurring, but it does not give reasons for the results. The translation of this information into usable data will require further analysis. For example, the realities of the internal organization, the performance of the various subsystems (eg, the availability of human and material resources) will have to be taken into consideration.

Consideration must also to be given to factors in the external environment that might have influenced performance. Thus, both quantitative and qualitative analyses will be required as part of the management control activity.

Taking Corrective Action

This is the final and critical stage in the control process. After clearly defined goals and objectives have been set, methods of measurement are determined, mechanisms for feedback are in place and systems to measure results against plans are established, then managers have the task of correcting deficiencies. Where 'actual' results are above the 'planned' results, managerial intervention is also required to re-examine the plan to determine whether positive changes ought to be made to future projections.

Analysis for corrective action should be based on the 'systems approach' to management and a SWOT (strengths, weaknesses, opportunities and threats) analysis could be used to ascertain whether the variations identified are the results of internal or external factors.

Performance Appraisal

This is the element of the control function that is concerned with reviewing and appraising the performance of people. Although theoretically, the basic control function focuses on achievement of objectives, these activities are performed by people, and the results achieved may be directly related to their abilities and capabilities. In the development of behavioral theories, the humanists have also placed some emphasis on the role of human motivation in the 'input-output' matrix.

Reasons for Appraisal

A priority reason for the formal appraisal of staff is to identify current levels of the performance of the employee, as well as his or her strengths and weaknesses. Appraisal is also used as a basis on which to reward individuals for their contribution to the organization's goals as well as to motivate them towards higher levels of performance. In this process, the potential for upward mobility can be identified and employees with potential can be selected for further training and development. Performance appraisals can benefit the organization as it can provide information to be used in succession planning.

These general reasons for appraisal are in tandem with the concept of Management by Objective, proposed by Peter Drucker and incorporated by Douglas McGregor in his development of a Theory Y approach to management. This approach is the opposite of Management by Control. The whole purpose of appraisal or evaluation should be to take corrective action where necessary and to use the information gathered from the review to formulate plans for the future. The employees must be aware of the reasons for evaluation, which should not be conceived as a punitive measure.

Methods of Appraisal

There are several methods used in organizations to appraise employees' performance. Appraisal methods have evolved over time from the traditional (mechanistic) top-down to a participative method. The traditional method was based solely on such generalized factors as personality, attributives and abilities such as leadership, initiative and judgement, rather than on performance on the job. The 'box-ticking' method, which lacks objectivity, did not provide a sound basis on which to make managerial decisions with respect to the reasons for appraisal.

Since the 1960s, there has been a shift towards a result-oriented approach based on performance standards in which job duties and responsibilities are being used. This approach allows the manager to apply measureable inertia to the assessment of employees' performance in a fair and more accurate manner.

An effective performance appraisal system must be based firstly on good communication between manager and employee. The objectives to be achieved must be clear, the criteria for measuring performance must be stated and specific times must be set for appraisal. Meetings should be held periodically, so that employees can discuss any problems that may arise. Appraisal times should range between short-, medium- or long term so that deviations may be detected early in the process of implementation.

One technique for appraising employees' performance is the 'critical incident' method. In this method, the manager keeps a record of all the critical incidents—whether positive or negative—that occur in the course of the employee's job performance. These incidents are linked to the 'critical job requirements' and, at the scheduled appraisal time, a tally of the critical incidents are used to assess the employee's performance.

In addition to the appraisal of individual performance, the control system should also include a system of rewards. The neoclassical and human relations theorists state that the satisfaction of some needs is integral to human motivation. Rewards may be extrinsic, such as pay increases, commissions and productivity allowance.

A manager may not be in a position to offer material incentives but can search for creative ways to satisfy higher-level needs by providing some intrinsic rewards such as recognition in the form of special awards, giving job satisfaction through job enrichment. These methods have to be individualized as each employee is at a different level of motivational need.

Limitations to Performance Appraisal

A manager with responsibility for appraising an employee's performance has to be aware of the difficulty in achieving objectivity in performance of this control activity. A limited number of these are given below:

- In large operations, it is difficult to appraise the performance of employees whose jobs are dependent on the support of several others for the satisfactory completion of tasks.

- In some service areas, there is often a conflict in establishing a balance between effectiveness (client satisfaction) and efficiency (economy in use of resources). In these areas, there could be a problem in determining whether to apply quantitative or qualitative measures on output.

- Environmental factors over which the employee has no control can have a negative effect on an individual's performance.

- Resource insufficiency (human and material) and differences in motivation among group members are factors in the organization environment over which individuals have no control.

- The human element: psychological and socio-psychological factors that influence an employee's tendency to inflate assessment of his or her own performance. This is usually the case where there is a fear factor related to the outcome of the appraisal.

As a manager moves his leadership towards a more participative style, many of the problems and limitations will become more obvious and more effectiveness in performance appraisal can be achieved.

The limitations can only be removed (or at least reduced) where the appraisal is conducted in an environment of trust and confidence in which employees have confidence in the appraisal method and there is opportunity for two-way feedback.

Skills Required to Perform Control Function

To be effective in performing the control function, a manager should be competent in the following activities:

- Setting targets for outputs
- Establishing standards of performance of individuals, groups and the organization
- Determining strategic points of control
- Designing and using information systems
- Analysing data
- Giving and receiving feedback
- Identifying deviations from plans
- Correcting deviations or revising plans in a timely manner.

Summary

Control as a management function completes the management cycle, which starts with planning. Effective control requires that standards be set against which performance should be measured. In control measurement, there must be uniformity between the standards or goals that are set and the standards used to measure the achievement. The time for measuring the frequency and the level of accuracy required should also be set.

A system for receiving feedback from both formal and informal sources will facilitate the process of control by comparing the relationship between planned and actual results. The control process is complete when action is taken to correct deviations and/or make any relevant changes to the plan.

Performance appraisal is an important element in the control function. It is concerned with the review performance of people and can serve the interest of individuals as well as the organization. Several different methods of appraising employee performance have developed over time, and all have inherent limitations. Managers who have responsibility for appraising employees' performance have to be aware of them and develop methods to improve effectiveness in the performance appraisal system.

References

Cole, G.A (2003) *Management: Theory & Practice*, op. cit, chaps. 28 & 29, pp. 246-263 (Cengage Learning EMEA).

Hampton, David (1981) "The Concept of Controls", in *Contemporary Management*, op. cit (McGraw-Hill, New York).

Hellriegel, Don & Slocum, John W. (1997) *Management* 4th ed., pp. 598-611 (Addison-Wesley Publications, Massachusetts).

Lawler, Edward E. & Rhodes, John G. (1976) *Information and Control in Organizations* (Goodyear Publishing Co. Inc., Pacific Palisades, California).

Strauss, George & Sayles, Leonard R. (1980) "Performance Appraisal and Management by Objectives", in *Personnel: The Human Problems of Management*. op. cit, chap, 23 (Prentice Hall, New York).

Online Resources

Performance Appraisal. Archer North & Associates, http://www.mindtools.com/pages/article/newLDR_98.htm.

Segal, Jonathan A. (2011, January 14) The Dirty Dozen Performance Appraisal Errors. Bloomberg Businessweek (online), http://www.businessweek.com/managing/content/jan2011/ca20110114_156455.htm.

Managing Time

Introduction

One writer on the subject of time management raised the following issues:

> "In management courses, why has the management of time been neglected? Of all resources time appears to be the least understood and the most mismanaged. We seem to have left the ultimate disposal of a priceless commodity unplanned and uncontrolled, subject to the vagaries of change" (Mackenzie op cit, 1972, p.3).

This statement points to the absence of any well-developed theory of 'time management'. The earliest attention given to the relationship between time and productivity was by the scientific management theorists. In this period (early 20th century) time and motion studies were applied to the performance of manual workers, and later, through the organization and methods (O&M) approach, to clerical workers. As organizations became more complex and the activities of individuals and groups became more interdependent, less emphasis was placed on the use of time as fundamental to the efficiency of individuals and, consequently, of the organization.

Since the early 1960s, writers have been offering time management guides, tips and suggestions to managers and professionals.

Definition of Time

Time has been defined in management literature as a resource, along with money, raw materials and information. Unlike the other resources, however, time is unique: it cannot be contained or held back; it cannot be stock-piled like raw material; it cannot be accumulated like money; it cannot be placed on deposit for future use. Time is an exact resource. There are exactly

- 24 hours in a day
- 168 hours in a week
- 8736 hours in a year

No more, no less. Everyone has the same amount of time—rich or poor, the powerful and the weak, the company president, the salesman, the ancillary worker, the housewife, the student and the unemployed, all have the same amount of time.

Another reality about the use of time is that some people achieve much more than others with the same amount of time. It has been argued, therefore, that time management is not necessarily a matter of having enough time, but rather a matter of managing the things that are done in that block of 168 hours per week. In other words, it is a matter of managing oneself.

Categories of Time Use

The things that fall within the scope of an individual's need to manage time can be categorized as follows:

- Things that are important and urgent. These are things that must be done immediately because they are absolute necessities that have to be completed within a very limited time frame. Failure to meet a 'time deadline' could have serious repercussions for the organization and/or the individual.

- Things that are important but not urgent. These are things that ought to be done because they are a part of the job requirements, but the time frame for their completion is more flexible.

- Things that are neither urgent nor important. These things do occupy a large portion of an individual's time. They are aesthetics in which individuals engage for their own satisfaction, but that do not contribute materially to the achievement of any goals (eg, arranging the papers on the desk before starting the preparation of a paper to be presented at a conference at which you are the guest speaker. It has been said that 80 percent of the time used by individuals in organizations achieves only 20 percent of the overall objectives.

Identifying and categorizing the use of available time is a first step towards solving the time-management problem. It is important to differentiate between 'effective' and 'efficient' time management, because not all aspects of the use of time are within the individual's control. Effective time management will not always result in the achievement of all objectives, but efficient time management is making the 'best' use of the time available.

Factors Affecting the Use of Time

The following are the main factors that impact the effective/efficient use of organizational time:

- The nature of the job (ie, job content)

- The organizational environment (ie, the job context)

- The manager's personal attributes

The Nature of the Job
Every job has, within its content, factors that are the very fabric of the job situation. For example, job situations that involve frequent interactions with others can affect the rate and pace of activities and are sometimes referred to as 'time robbers'. Other

job situations include those with a high degree of 'crises', which requires a manager to make non-programmed decisions and can be time consuming.

The organization environment

The job context that is the environment in which work is done, presents one of the greatest challenges to effective time management. The internal organization includes the following:

- The structure of the organization (eg, the superior's control over information that can cause delay in the decision-making process).

- The subordinate's limited authority to take action that often results in the senior manager's loss of time spent in explaining simple processes.

- The policy environment, which includes the concept that the "customer is always right" provides the basis for customers' manipulation and insistence that managers spend inordinate amounts of time in solution of their specific problems.

Personal Attributes

A manager's basic personality can influence his or her ability to effectively manage time. Such traits as

- lack of assertiveness and fear of hurting the feelings of others;
- inability to communicate clearly, to express thoughts and ideas and to listen carefully or give feedback;
- lack of appropriate knowledge and understanding of the action required to efficiently complete tasks;
- inability to spend significant portions of time concentrating on a given task (ie, having a short attention span).

Among these sets of factors are some that fall outside the manager's control, while some others are referred to as 'time robbers' and can be effectively managed.

Strategies for Managing Time

The first step towards improving time management is conducting an analysis of how time is being used. One recommended method is to keep a time log or an activity analysis sheet. This process involves keeping, over a five-day period, a record of all job-related work and entering every activity on a chart and the length of time spent on each activity.

This record keeping, if done in detail, is one of the best ways of identifying the real 'time robbers', some of which often pass unnoticed. Some of the most obvious are

- too-long telephone calls;
- meetings of all kinds—scheduled and unscheduled;
- frequent interruptions by staff, superiors and colleagues, some of which often result from having an open-door policy; and
- unnecessary paperwork (eg, overuse of written communication when an oral message could be more effective).

Not everyone's time robbers are the same because each person's work situation is different. The time analysis chart will present a clearer picture of the major time wasters or time robbers. Some practical ideas for managing time would incorporate the elements or functions of management.

Planning time use

Having a time plan is basic to good time management. Without a plan, it would not be possible to evaluate whether time has been used efficiently. Time management plans should have short-, medium- and long-term focus. Time should be budgeted and its use reviewed regularly to measure whether the outputs are in keeping with the goals that were set out in the plan. It is important to include some 'slack time' to allow for unintended outcomes.

Organizing the use of time

In addition to a time plan, there should be an organizing technique. Tasks and activities should be arranged so that there will be maximum output from input of time. Because practical demands on a manager's time change from day to day, or even momentarily, a practical strategy is to have a 'to do' list to start each day. In this list, tasks should be placed in order of priority. Time, which is always at a premium, could be more effectively spent if the list is ordered to give priority to things that must be done before things that should be done. However, this is not a hard-and-fast rule, because sometimes things that are not considered important will change through circumstances and might become urgent.

The organizing and reorganizing of time requires skills in decision-making. Organizing time will involve others in the organization whose interests, needs and demands must also to be taken into consideration, and should be included in the priority list.

Organizing Others

Significant others who should be integrated into the organizing process and for whom time management techniques can be applied include the following:

Superiors

These person, who are sometimes referred to as 'the boss' can be time robbers because they have power to use formal authority to do so.

- One technique is to work away from the office for certain periods of time when there is an urgent task to be completed.

- To avoid time being wasted in meetings that are unstructured and too long, a signal should be given that there should be an agenda, or a request could be made for an early item on the agenda because of another previous urgent engagement.

Colleagues

Where these individuals are identified as time robbers, time-management strategies could include the following:

- Avoid asking trivial questions of drop-in visitors.

- Remove extra seating in your work space.

- Control use of the open-door policy by setting specific times for access, and be gracefully firm when refusing unscheduled visits.

Clients

The importance of clients to a manager's business cannot be overstressed. However, the same techniques that apply to colleagues should also apply to clients. Whereas good interpersonal relationships with clients are critical for business, they should not be allowed to exploit this situation by making unscheduled visits. Some strategies for avoiding time wasting by clients include the following:

- Where possible, have someone screen telephone calls and make appointments.

- Keep the office door closed, and do not answer the first rap on the door —this will give the impression that you are really busy.

- Post a notice of office hours on your door.

- Request a brief account of the purpose of a scheduled visit to avoid a long preamble and to signal a desire to stay within time limit.

These are some techniques that anyone desiring to be an effective time manager can apply. Needless to say, these strategies will not always have the desired effect but, without a plan and a structure for organizing time, the manager's time cannot be efficiently utilized.

Controlling Time Use

This process involves evaluating the use of time on a timely basis.

- At the end of a day, an examination of the 'to do' list is a practical form of control. Tasks that have not been completed can be rolled over and become a part of the plan for the following day, or postponed where it is more practical to do so.

- A review of the activity analysis sheet will expose the time robbers who should be placed on notice to be eliminated as far as is possible.

- The daily diary is also an excellent control tool. Important appointments that had to be postponed should be rescheduled as soon as possible.

- A re-examination should be conducted of the categories of those things that fall within the scope of the need to manage time and create a new list, using the daily 'to do' list and the monthly or annual diary as a master plan.

General Principles of Time Management

- *Practice punctuality.* Being on time for appointments is a 'no-fail' way of saving time. At the same time, always have a plan to use 'slack time' productively in case others are not punctual.

- *Do not procrastinate.* It has been said that "procrastination is the thief of time". The axiom "never put off for tomorrow what can be done today" is a useful tip for time management.

- *Learn to say 'No.'* Being able to say no to the temptation to participate in image-building activities can be very useful in managing time. While some social activities are essential to maintaining a balanced life, over-commitment to the demands of others can be an obstacle to efficient job performance, as well as maintaining of good medical health.

Summary and Conclusions

The management of time is an important element in the process of management. Time is a resource that, if not efficiently and effectively managed, can have a negative effect on the other management functions.

Being aware of the factors that are obstacles to good time management (time robbers) is a first step towards the development of strategies and techniques of time management. The elements of management that are employed in the management of all other organizational resources can also be employed in this process. Every manager has different time-management problems but they can be solved by thinking critically and making use of decision-making, planning, organizing and controlling techniques.

References

Armstrong, Michael (1988) *How to be an Even Better Manager,* 2nd ed. pp.311-324 (Nicholas Publishing Co., New York).

Cole, Diane (September 1986) "Ten Time Management Tips", in *Essence*, p. 130.

Cole, G.A. (1993) *Management: Theory and Practice*, op cit. chap 25 (DP Publications, London).

Drucker, Peter (April 1961) "How to be an Effective Executive", in *Nations Business* (Chamber of Commerce of the United States of America, Washington, D.C.)

Johns, Ted (1994) *Perfect Time Management: All you Need to Get it Right the First Time* (Arrow Books, London).

McKenzie, R. Alex (1972) *The Time Trap: Managing Your Way Out* (American Management Association Inc., New York).

Managing Change

Introduction

In the overview of the historical development of management thought, it was seen that, throughout the ages, several changes in social and economic environments influenced the development of different theoretical perspectives on management. In the early stages, the theories evolved first along a nonrational trajectory and later on the basis of scientific research. In all these circumstances, the objective was to consciously manipulate the required resources (human and material) to achieve organizational efficiency and effectiveness.

Recognizing the inevitability of change in every human situation is one of the challenges that managers have always faced. The thought has repeatedly been expressed that "the only thing that is constant is change". Towards the end of the 20th century and into the 21st century, the rate and pace of change has been phenomenal, raising the question of whether change can really be managed.

Functions of the Change Manager

A change manager's responsibility is to utilize the management process to create situations in which organizational change takes place with minimum dislocation. This requires the manager to 'get out of the box', to move away from the tried and tested ways of doing things.

Change managers may approach the change process either reactively or proactively—these two approaches are two extremes at opposite ends of a continuum—and apply different methods to prevent the organization from falling into a state of disequilibrium.

The reactive change manager

Reactive changes take place in response to a situation that is 'bearing down' on the organization. The reactive change manager, for example, waits indifferently until there is notice served about an impending industrial action before recognizing the several signs of restiveness among staff , which could include

- increased number of resignations among long-standing members of staff, or

- increase in the number of complaints about the quality of life in the organization.

The reactive manager depends mainly on the 'carrot and stick' approach to solve problems that could have been solved before they occur. When faced with a problem, the reactive manager either applies sanctions or gives a reward.

The proactive change manager

As the term suggests, the proactive change manager anticipates problems, which are identified through research in other similar areas of operation, watches the market and scans the environment. This type of manager knows that "the sound of thunder is a sign of rain". While the manager recognizes that not all change is controllable, he or she must anticipate threats or challenges and be prepared to maximize the benefits of change, while minimizing the negative consequences. The proactive manager is flexible rather than rigid and seeks out problems rather than take the view that "what you don't know can hurt you".

Forces in the Change Process

All organizations exist in an environment in which forces within and outside their boundaries have an impact on their capacity to maintain equilibrium. The effective manager must be aware of the forces that are likely to affect the organization and develop strategies to respond to the changes in demands on the system.

External Forces

The external environment presents several challenges to a manager who would be a change agent: External forces include the following:

Consumers

These are actual or potential consumers, a diverse group with needs and wants to which the organization must respond in order to survive. Consumers may demand more, or better quality of the goods and services provided, or delivery at a faster rate. These are forces of change that a manager must recognize. Failure to do so could result in loss of business.

Competitors

Other companies or organizations in the same task environment are external forces that can be either a threat or a challenge. They can 'wean' away customers, reduce profits as well as reduce influence. On the other hand, competitors can provide opportunities for collaborative effort, which can help the organization to grow and expand.

The Legal System

As a change force, laws that are enacted can significantly affect the goals, policies and operations of an organization. As a country enters into new international agreements, new laws are sometimes enacted that, in turn, require changes to be made in operational practices within the organization.

Technology

This is a major force for change. The explosion in technological development since the last quarter of the 20th century has been the most pervasive of external forces. Automation in manufacturing, banking and finance, agricultural production and, most dramatically, in information technology has provided opportunities and challenges for the proactive manager, and has been a direct threat to the reactive manager.

Internal Forces

The input/output relationship between the organization and its external environment is a major factor creating demand for internal change. These internal forces include structural, technological and psychological.

Structural Forces

A bureaucratic organization structure itself is a force because it is usually based on rigid rules and procedures, standard operational practices which are not compatible with a dynamic environment. For example, a system of rewards that is based on fixed salaries and increments do not recognize or encourage higher levels of performance and productivity. Reform in administration and management that include such factors as the change in employment criteria is a structural force which can have an impact on the other internal forces, such as psychological forces.

Technologies Forces

This change force, also brought about by external forces, affects the need for different and, in some instances, more advanced levels of education and training. An organization that is going through a change process is required to change its methods of production, its equipment, employment policies etc. The balance of power between older and younger employees is another internal force that is stimulated by technological factors.

Democratization in Society

In general, the emergence of a less authoritarian society (in most developed and developing countries) has resulted in an increase in demand for a more democratic style of leadership in the workplace. This has caused some of the traditional concepts, such as strict hierarchical structure, impersonality, etc. to become obsolete. Consequently, some of the bases on which authority was legitimated in the past would have to be changed as new bases, which are more socially compatible, emerge.

Cultural Diversity

Another change force in the organization is the socio-cultural diversity that has emerged as a result of, inter alia, mass immigration. Certain norms, and values, which were considered sacrosanct have had to be abandoned and certain others, which were considered unacceptable, have had to be integrated into the culture of the organization. For example, standards of style of dress, social class and background, which were prescribed to meet the criteria of 'order', have to be changed to reduce conflict in organizations.

Psychological Forces

A combination of some or all the other internal forces can be a catalyst for the emergence of psychological forces. Because people make up the organization, the feelings, either expressed or suppressed, can be a force for change. The perception, expectations, attitude and behavior of employees can lead to negative action, which can, in turn, lead to negative outcomes that undermine the very changes being made. Increased absenteeism, frequent resignations of valuable employees as well as industrial action expressed through strikes or 'sick-outs' can force management to review and sometimes change their policies and practices.

Steps in the Change Process

In addition to knowing the forces that influence change, an effective manager knows that implementing change is not an easy task: it has to be done through a systematic process, which includes a number of steps.

Step 1 – Perception

Identification of a need for change may occur after a long period of insensitivity to the obvious need or it can occur as a sudden 'bright' idea. The idea of the need for change can come from any source, likely or unlikely, but without recognition or perception of a need for change, nothing will happen.

Step 2 – Search for Solution

Having positively identified a need for change, the next step is to search for alternative ways of approaching the need problem. The search for a solution should follow a rational decision-making path, which should include a decision about the outcome of the change that is desired. The process should take into consideration as many alternative ways of solving the existing problem as possible and should include as many persons as possible who would be affected by the proposed change. This is the stage at which staff motivation can increase as their social and ego needs are met through participation.

Step 3 – Evaluate the ideas or suggestions

At this stage, the anticipation of outcomes must take into consideration the fact that all outcomes will be in the future and there can be no absolute certainty about the future state of things. The evaluation process should, therefore, incorporate ideas from those who will be affected by the outcome of the change. Participants also should have an opportunity to see the value of their inputs in their discussion. The process should allow all contributors to the 'basket of ideas' an opportunity to discuss the possible costs as well as benefits of each idea. The selection of the alternative should follow "the law of the situation" (Follet) and bear in mind that the goal is to find a solution that is likely to give the highest net benefit.

Step 4 – Implement the Change

The implementation of change must be managed in the same way any routine organization problem is managed. The difference, however, is that change activities are likely to put the organization into a state of disequilibrium in the short run, and requires careful monitoring to ensure that individuals do not revert to their accustomed methods of doing things. The change manager must bear in mind that full participation and agreement at the previous stages do not guarantee success in implementation. The manager must follow up with constant monitoring and controlling until the process achieves a 'steady slate'.

Resistance to Change

While change is not only an inevitable but also a desirable feature in the management process, the task of managing change is not always accepted. Change can be a challenge to both management as well as non-management personnel. Both categories may regard change as a personal threat and develop their own methods of resisting change. The reasons for resistance to change may be as varied as the persons who occupy positions in the organization. Some of these reasons are as follows:

Misunderstanding of the change
If people do not understand the nature of the change or have inaccurate perceptions, they may erroneously believe that there are some hidden agendas in the process.

Negative responses to disruptions
This occurs when change requires individuals to change the daily routine to which they have become accustomed. For example, changes that disrupt family life, recreation activities, or any other psychological attachments that have meaning can be a reason for resistance.

Fear of material or non-material loss
This resistance is based on the perception that personal costs of the change will be more than the benefits. If an employee believes that a change will result in loss of salary or any other monetary reward or, if there is a feeling that there is a lowering of personal status, there will be resistance. There also will be resistance to any change that is perceived to lead to an increased workload without additional compensation.

Low tolerance for change
Some individuals have more difficulty dealing with change than others. This could be due to low self-confidence, an aversion to risk or low tolerance or any form of disruption. Change may be resisted if an officer refuses, or is unable to relinquish, the tasks of a previous job by taking them along to a new position. This action will not yield the desired effectiveness of the change.

Managerial indecisiveness
A manager might create a barrier to change through hesitation in implementing the new ideas. By verbally expressing doubt about possible outcomes he or she could also cause a negative response on the part of subordinates.

Forms of Resistance to Change

In addition to knowing why people resist change, a manager has to be aware of the methods that he or she will employ to resist change. Even those who verbally agree to change may also resist change when it comes to the implementation stage, and the forms of resistance may be either overt or subtle. They may include the following:

Open challenges
These come from those who openly disagree with the proposed change, while some have second thoughts about something with which they had previously agreed. This

approach does not necessarily mean that the objector will win or lose their arguments: there is always a possibility that some form of conflict resolution can be used to create a positive solution.

Subtle resistance

This form of resistance is more difficult to manage, because the problem can only be recognized by symptoms rather than by concrete evidence of the real problem. Disappearance of documents, unusually frequent breakdown of machinery and abnormally frequent staff absences can be subtle methods used to resist change.

Staff representation

The growth of staff associations and the development of trade union movements can be a form of resistance to change. This occurs where informal groups feel that a change will not work to their advantage. The process may start slowly with restiveness and build up to a point where management has to divert energy towards settlement of disputes rather than implement the change.

Structural resistance

In general, the formal structure of organization is established to ensure stability, predictability and uniformity. Attempts to use the same structure to innovate and make changes in the organization are likely to meet resistance. Any change that threatens the status quo (eg, promotion on merit vs. by seniority, legitimization of authority on the basis of technical competence vs. formal position) will surely meet resistance by those who were the beneficiaries of the existing norm.

Techniques for Managing Change

The management of change is one of the more difficult tasks a manager will be required to perform. In addition to the various forms that resistance to change might take, the manager as change agent must have a real commitment to change, which could also be a threat to his or her own stability. It has been stated that "to be an agent of change, a manager must first change himself". This might require the manager to be committed to changing old habits and old ways of doing things.

Managing change involves three basic elements of the management process: structure, technology and personnel.

Structure

The introduction of change in the organization will require modifications to the following structural features:

- division of labour/specialization
- authority structure/chain of command
- levels of centralization and decentralization
- span of control
- depth of structure—tall vs. flat.

In implementing change, managers are required to alter these basic structural features to meet the needs of the proposed changes. Structural changes can be very disruptive because of their impact on the routines of people who work in the organization.

Technology

The function of technology in the management process is to transform inputs into outputs. The technology includes the knowledge and skills, work processes and equipment used in this process. Change in technology is self-propelling and change managers have to be aware of advances in technological development and seek to apply them to the production processes. Technological changes will also include the employment of new categories of personnel and retraining of existing staff.

Technological changes also require the manager to acquire more appropriate technology, as the situation requires. Among the most advanced and rapidly changing technology is the evolution in automation and the use of the computer. Change managers also have to become more skilled in the use of the new technology.

Human Resources

This is the element of change that involves changing the attitudes, perception, motivation and behavior of people. This is the most intractable aspect of the change process and will require the active intervention of managers at every stage of the change process. Structural and technological changes will impact on the psycho-social system and bring about changes in people whose ways of doing things, their well-being and other non-material factors will be disrupted.

Techniques or programmes intended to change people were developed in the human relations schools of thought, and experts in the field of organization development (OD) have developed techniques to change people, in an effort to improve the quality of interpersonal relations. Following are a few of these programmes:

Team building

In this process members are assisted through group interaction to develop new attitudes to their working group and to be more open and trusting. This approach helps to break down the traditional culture of individuality and competition for scarce resources which formal organizations tend to encourage.

Sensitivity training

This method is used to change attitudes and behavior among and between groups. It involves the use of professionals trained in the behavioral sciences, whose role is to help provide an environment in which individuals can react and respond freely without set guidelines. The professional does not perform a leadership role, but allows participants to express their feelings on any subject of their choice.

The main objective of this change technique is to help individuals to develop their communications skills. Although this method has been in use for some time, the overall effectiveness in bringing about long-term results, especially in the area of job performance, is still unknown. However, some short-term gains have been made in areas of communication, perception and participative efforts.

Process consultation

Another technique for change is one in which the focus is on the manager. The role of the consultant is to act as a coach to assist the manager to "perceive, understand and act on the process problems". This technique helps change managers who have become overwhelmed by the different aspects of the management process and spend more time 'fire-fighting' than engaged in actual problem-solving.

A process consultation can help the manager to find experts in the field of human resources management who can assist in solving specific problems.

Summary and Conclusions

Change is a universal fact of life. It takes place whether it is recognized or not. There can be no growth or development without change. The approaches to the management of change may be either to wait until something happens and react to it (reactive approach) or plan ahead for change, taking into consideration the possibilities and probabilities that a particular kind of change will occur (the proactive approach).

A manager must be aware of the fact that there are several environmental forces— external or internal—that have an impact on change, and be aware of the possible effects of these change forces on the organization. The stages in the change process are identified as perception, search for solution, evaluation, selection and implementation.

The manager's best guide to managing change is knowledge of the various reasons why people resist change and the forms that resistance takes. This knowledge is invaluable if a manager is to respond proactively and avoid unnecessary dislocations.

There are a number of tried and tested techniques for managing change, mainly in areas of structure, technology and human resources management. These techniques have met varied levels of success, mainly because of the mercurial nature of change. It has been said that "the only constant thing about change is that it is constant" (see Robbins and Coulter p. 393). Managing change can be both challenging and rewarding. For the creative manager it is a constant source of intellectual stimulation.

References

Drucker, Peter (1995) "The New Society of Organization", in *Managing in a Time of Great Chance* (Penguin Books Ltd., London)

Lupthans, Fred (1977) "Organization Development", in *Organizational Behaviour*, 2nd ed., chap. 21 (McGraw Hill, Kogakusha Ltd, London).

Montana, Patrick J. & Charnov, Bruce (2008) "Managing Organization Change", in *Management* 2nd ed., pp. 301- 314 (Barron's Educational Series, New York).

Robbins, Stephen P. & Coulter, Mary (2002) "Managing Change and Innovation", in *Management*, 6th ed. op. cit., chap. 12 (Prentice Hall, New York).

Strauss, George & Sayles, Leonard R. (1980): "Introducing Change: The Managerial Issues", in *Personnel—The Human Problems of Management*, 4th ed. chap. 10. (Prentice Hall International, Inc.)

Toffler, Alvin (1960) *The Third Wave.* (Morrow, New York).

Toffler, Alvin (1970) *Future Shock* (Banton Books, New York).

" Dr. Barrett has integrated

these variables well while

writing a valuable text that

offers strategies and examples

to address managerial and

administrative issues relevant

to any setting. This is a timeless

work, which will be valuable to

students pursuing any aspect of

management or administration,

in any setting or environment,

while challenging the student

and/or manager to develop

new thoughts and ideas about

the management of formal

organizations. "

Hermi H. Hewitt
OD, PhD, RN, RM, FAAN

Ina Barrett, PhD, educator and writer, has lectured and written on public administration and organizational and human resource management at the University of the West Indies for over 30 years. She is also author of *Organizational Challenges: A Caribbean Perspective*, a case book. Dr. Barrett has served as consultant in health and public service management to several Caribbean governments and regional and international organizations. In 2011, she was honoured with an award for distinguished services to the International Association of Schools and Institutes of Administration at their 50th anniversary conference, held in Rome, Italy.

Book Design: Carole Thompson